D1410886

The Power of Logos

The
Power *of* Logos

How to Create Effective
Company Logos

William L. Haig
&
Laurel Harper

A VNR Book

JOHN WILEY & SONS, INC.

New York   Chichester   Weinheim   Brisbane   Singapore   Toronto

This publication is designed to provide accurate and authoritative information in regard to the subject matter covered. It is sold with the understanding that the publisher is not engaged in rendering professional services. If professional advice or other expert assistance is required, the services of a competent professional person should be sought.

Library of Congress Cataloging-in-Publication Data:

Haig, William L.
    The power of logos: how to create effective company logos / William L.
Haig, Laurel Harper.
        p.   cm.
    Includes bibliographical references and index.
    ISBN 0-471-28778-4
    1. Corporate image.   2. Logos (Symbols).   I. Harper, Laurel.
II. Title
HD59.2.H35   1997
659.2'85—dc21   94-49074
                                                                                CIP

Printed in the United States of America

10   9   8   7   6   5   4   3

Contents

Foreword

The process of doing an identity is one of the most challenging design projects you can undertake. I read something not long ago in *Adobe* magazine, written by Anistatia Miller and Jared Brown, that pretty much sums it up. In essence, it said:

> A CEO was meeting with a designer and a writer about refashioning his company's image. He told the writer to create a brochure telling what the company was about, where it came from, and where it was going. He should do it in 3000 words, and not worry too much about what he said as he could change it next quarter. Then the CEO turned to the designer. He told her that she, too, must do basically the same thing as the writer. Only she must convey her message by creating one little symbol that would be seen by a hundred times more people. Oh—and it must last forever.

That's what you face all the time.

An identity is the absolute bare-bones representation of a company. By definition it has to be simple. You must be able to enlarge it and apply it to the side of a truck or a building; it has to emboss beautifully on a business card; work well on uniforms; and service a wide range of applications. It has to endure all these execution requirements.

In addition, a great logo does more than just portray the current company image and statement. We create a logo or mark that the company can also grow into. It's an identity, not a spot illustration or a photo or a moving picture. And when a designer creates a logo, he or she has an obligation to create something appropriate that becomes the visual voice of what that company or product is— something that reflects the credibility of that company. At the same time, it must be unique and aesthetically pleasing. You can do something that is appropriate but unappealing, or beautiful but inappropriate. You must satisfy all three things to really hit that grand slam. Simplicity, ultimately, is what usually plays out.

To do this involves a lot of back-and-forth with the client, a hand-in-glove relationship; it's a balance the client must play a part in. Yet, logos have become like designer labels on the backs of jeans—people (i.e., clients) feel like they can change them whenever the desire hits, and it shouldn't take a lot of time to do one. There are still those businesspeople who understand the potency of a good logo, but the general businessperson treats them with a lot less reverence than they used to. It's impossible for them to not look at the large or successful companies whose identities have held true as the companies themselves have ebbed and flowed, and their product mixes have changed, and say, "Boy, that's really important to have one of those. I want one."

Yet, they don't understand what's involved in doing a truly successful logo. It appears that there are some designers who feel the same. They just want to sit down at their computers and start designing. They don't want to take the time to do what proves critical to the success of any company identity—researching that company or product to find out what is at the heart of its business style; what its personality is all about; and what is the soul of the company. Yet without taking the time to uncover what makes that company tick, there is no way you can ever hope to create a mark that will adequately and truthfully represent it.

Without discovering what makes that company credible in its field, then ensuring that you incorporate these traits into their logo design, you are only cheating your client and their public. And, ultimately, you'll not be providing your client with its full potential.

Jack Anderson
Hornall Anderson Design Works

Preface

The Power of Company Imagery

One of the most essential components of any business' marketing program, its logo, can be one of the most overlooked. Many companies think nothing of investing thousands and thousands of dollars in advertising campaigns, yet when it comes down to sinking money into developing an effective, attractive logo, they get cold feet.

That is a bad business decision.

Even more than advertising, a logo works for a company in numerous ways. The public encounters hundreds of logo impressions each day, in every form, from stationery, business cards, and invoices, to television and print ads, signage, company vehicles, and brochures, to name just a few. All are highly visible—and potentially cost-efficient—forms of public contact. That's why astute companies from Nike to Coca-Cola to Prudential work hard to ensure they have developed a powerful logo that fits their image, plus meets the demands of their marketing program.

A small family-owned company has a relatively easy time communicating its image, usually taking on the personality of its owner, for better or worse. But as a company grows in size, so do its communication problems. Every company, also for better or for worse, projects an image through its graphics program. If enough money is spent promoting it, probably any logo can achieve an identity and recognition factor for its company. However, unless the logo promotes the business as credible, you may as well throw those dollars spent developing it out the window. It can actually send the wrong message, a fuzzy message, or no message. It's the same as wasting money on a poorly conceived advertising campaign. At the same time, planning, creating, and implementing a logo that

P–1

P–2

incorporates credibility persuasion attributes might just be one of the best investments a company will ever make.

A vigorous corporation and a dynamic company graphics program often go hand-in-hand. Companies like United Airlines and Xerox quickly come to mind (Figures P–1 and P–2). Such major corporations employ their company logos as marketing communication tools. So does Joe's Barber Shop, although probably in a much more limited manner than the conglomerates. Still, there is no reason that even a small business can't get much value from a well-designed logo, if it follows the lead of its large counterparts.

Such companies are on the leading edge of their fields, and look that way through **graphic design** (text and/or various icons arranged in a manner that facilitates the conveyance of their messages) because they recognize design's importance not as just a form of art, but as a *marketing tool.*

Design's main purpose and power is to influence or motivate. Its power extends to a company's products, too. Why did *USA Today* gain such a large circulation, practically overnight, when local newspapers already covered most of the same information, many times much more in-depth? It's because the design makes *USA Today* enticing and easy to read. It was a breakthrough in newspaper graphics, an experiment that paid off big for its trailblazing owners.

Since the mid 1960s, design's role as a powerful marketing tool has steadily gained ground. The concepts of **corporate identity** and **corporate imagery** have become part of a smart business's marketing mix. Any company's success will depend, to a considerable extent, on establishing a favorable interface between its business and its various publics. The logo can be a significant factor in achieving that aim.

An article in a March 1991 issue of *Fortune* magazine, titled "Design that Sells and Sells and . . .," states:

> Many American corporations are embracing design as the hot strategic tool for the 1990s. Many corporations have improved operations to the point where they can match each other on price, quality, and technology. How, then, to differentiate yourself? Says Robert Hays at the Harvard Business School, "Fifteen years ago companies competed on price. Today it's quality. Tomorrow it's design."

The logo is the heart and soul of a business' design persona. It's imperative, then, that it be imbued with the essence and strength of the company or product that it defines. As the designer, it's up to you to ensure this prime objective is satisfied.

But how do you achieve logo power? It's a matter of defining the company's character and attributes, discovering what sets it apart from the competition, and determining its goals. Then you must translate all those elements visually into an icon that helps achieve the company's objectives. Logo power is likewise the product of a symbiotic relationship between graphic designer and client, a process at the heart of which is *total* communication and, therefore, total understanding of one another's objectives and responsibilities.

Credibility-based logo power is the communication future of both small and large businesses, nationally and internationally. But it's a future that will be much brighter when the company manager and graphic designer share this visual literacy, then use it to work together in creating expressive, intelligent logos.

Acknowledgments

The late Saul Bass is generally recognized as the greatest graphic designer of our time. More than a designer, he was a great communicator. His teachings inspired the discovery of the credibility persuasion principle in communication as the basis for logo planning and design. The power of the company logo is now clearly understood in simple terms. The authors wish to thank Saul Bass for the gift which is the essence of this book.

The authors wish to thank all the talented designers who participated in this book, without whose help it would not have been possible to accomplish. A special thanks to Jack Anderson, Jim Cross, Debra Kelley, Charles Anderson, and Malcolm Grear for sharing their insight into the identity design and planning process, and to Joel Grear, Scott Plunkett (Chermayeff & Geismar, Inc.), Christina Arbini (Hornall Anderson Design Works), and Wendy Wenzel (Bass Yager Associates) for fielding our numerous calls and faxes, and for their fast response to our many requests.

Additionally, we want to extend a very special thanks to editors Jane Degenhardt and Beth Harrison at Van Nostrand Reinhold for all their patience and assistance, and to Bud Linschoten for his design advice throughout the process of developing this book. And, last but not least, a very special thanks to our families, especially Laurel's husband George Harper, and Bob and Joann Hoskins (Dad and Mom), who had to endure all Laurel's whining while she was on deadline.

Bill's sons Chris and Zane Haig, and daughter Cristi Prince are the legacy to a better, more understandable world. Mother Margery and father Paul Haig are always to be remembered for pursuing the "why in life" until there is meaning.

The Power of Logos

1

IN A NUTSHELL

- Logos have existed for centuries, but truly began to emerge as the heart of the corporate identity program in the 1950s.

- Nonverbal communication accounts for 65 percent of our daily communication experiences. We continually interpret nonverbal cues to help us understand the world in which we live. The logo is one of business' most "outspoken" nonverbal cues.

- Logo power occurs when the logo is designed and implemented so that it establishes immediate, credible recognition for the client; expresses the client's character or attitude; conveys that the client is an expert or leader in its field; symbolizes the line of business; is a value qualifier for that client; is so memorable it becomes a unique visual identifier that is synonymous with the client's business; and it becomes an endorsement of that client's product, organization, or service.

As people, we learned to talk and be heard in order to serve our needs. And like people, businesses need to have an effective voice to achieve their goals. That's especially true in this age of electronic communications. We have become an information society, with the gathering and dissemination of information being a mighty armament for any business. The importance of communications in business today is beyond dispute.

That's where logos come in. Logos are not decoration. Logos define the company business. Logos define the company personality. Logos are image and substance, concurrently. The logo has been called the epitome of a company's entire communications system. Thus it follows that if the *business* of business is communications, and the company logo is at the heart of marketing communications,

FIGURE 1–1. *Lucent Magazine is distributed monthly to 230,000 worldwide employees of Lucent Technologies Inc. The logotype is a variation on the OCR and Triplex fonts, rendered to suggest the "glowing with light" interpretation of the word* lucent, *while the background is created from the word* people *repeated in multiple translations.*

it is incumbent that companies learn how logos work to unleash their full power. And it is imcumbent that designers know how to develop a logo that is imbued with such power.

It is not hard to find a graphic designer who can develop an attractive logo. However, it is difficult to find one who understands how to create a logo that not only looks good, but is a visual articulation of the client's *credibility*—in other words, a believable and trustworthy representation of its company—and, ultimately, reflects its expertise which is the product's service nature and the spirit of the company as well (Figure 1–1).

It is even more difficult to find a company leader who understands how powerful the logo can be as a marketing tool. Frank Stanton of CBS; Tom Watson, Jr., IBM; Hans and Florence Knoll of Knoll furniture; Walter Paepcke, Container Corporation of America; Adriano Olivetti of Olivetti; D. C. Burnham, Westinghouse; and Peter McColough, Xerox, all had one thing in common, aside from being powerful leaders of corporate giants: They understood the value of logos and graphic design in their marketing programs. And the success of their respective companies under their tenures backs up this thinking.

But where are such leaders today? Several corporations that once relied heavily on graphics as a marketing tool have become careless and even some designers are claiming the logo is no longer the marrow of a corporate design program. Yet look at Nike, AT&T, Apple, and their ilk. What do you think of the second their name is mentioned? If you're like the majority of the world, it's their logo in conjunction with their business. That, alone, should put the logo's importance in perspective.

A Short History of the Logo

Logos have been in existence for centuries. In a way, even your family's coat of arms can be considered one. Some of the earliest business applications of logos can be traced back to medieval days, when guilds employed them to control trade. By the 1700s, nearly every trader or dealer had his own mark. But it wasn't until the twentieth century that futuristic company leaders came to recognize that design, employed in everything from graphics programs to product forms, could be a very powerful tool in helping position their companies as market leaders.

In the 1950s, the logo truly began to come into its own, venturing far beyond a mere identification mark. James K. Fogleman, who in 1951 became design director of CIBA (the American subsidiary of Basel's Society for Chemical Industry), was among the first to actively urge designers and corporations to strive for a **corporate identity**. He defined corporate identity as a "controlled visual expression" of the company's character and personality. Still, the thrust of Fogleman's program was not in the logo itself, but the *application* of the logo throughout all the company's graphics.

At the same time, such designers as Paul Rand focused on developing strong, memorable logos as the very heart of a corporation's identity program. Heavily influenced by architecture and European typographic design, Rand's work is characterized by wit, simplicity, and a Bauhaus approach to problem solving. His marks are often driven by both the architect's quest for long-lasting functionality and New Typography's legibility and clean lines.

One of the best examples of his success is the logo he developed for International Business Machines. By the middle of the twentieth century, IBM had grown from a company that produced tabulating

FIGURE 1–2. *The IBM logo, designed in 1956 by Paul Rand, conveyed the company's prime business by suggesting the letters from a typewriter. At the same time it retained much of the equity of the original logo.*

FIGURE 1–3. An update by Rand in 1960 striped it to suggest scan lines and convey IBM's continuing advancements into technology. It has required little modification since.

FIGURE 1–4. IBM carefully guards the integrity of its logo, employing not just a standards manual (seen here), but a program manager of corporate identity and design. (IBM and the IBM logotype are registered trademarks of International Business Machines Corporation.)

machines, computing scales, and time recorders when it formed in 1911 (as the Computing-Tabulating-Recording Company) in a merger, to an innovative manufacturer of, first, typewriters, then in 1944, computers. Though clearly a leader in its field, IBM chairman Thomas Watson Jr. was impressed by the design work being done by rival Olivetti. He was concerned that IBM's own design program wasn't more distinguished. So, in 1956, he commissioned Rand to create a mark that would express the "extremely advanced and up-to-date nature of IBM's products." Rand complied by squaring the holes in the existing logo's "B" and making serifs on all three letters to match, playing off the letters made by a typewriter. Rand later said that he didn't want to stray too far from the firm's existing conservative mark, as conservatism was the nature of the company, yet his creation (Figure 1–2) not only fulfilled IBM's dictums, but was flexible enough that it has had the mark of true logo success—longevity. In the decades since its development, the logo has required only minor alterations, such as when Rand added stripes (Figure 1–3) to his original design, both to add interest and to reflect new technological advances (Figure 1–4).

The success of IBM and other such corporate innovators was finally getting through to the mass business audience that a well-developed logo could be a compelling marketing asset. For instance, Saul Bass Associates' mark update for Bell Telephone (Figure 1–5), designed in 1969, increased that company's recognition factor by 19 percent within a two-year period. In 1984, Bass's new mark (Figure 1–6) played a vital role in repositioning AT&T (which recently had split from Bell) from a national telephone business to a global communications power. And Chermayeff & Geismar Inc.'s logo for Chase Manhattan Bank, developed in 1959,

FIGURE 1–5. *The creation of the famous Bell symbol is attributed to AT&T General Manager Angus Hibbard, back in 1889. When AT&T took over the Bell company in 1899, it applied its bell symbol to that division. In 1969, Saul Bass Associates updated the existing version of the bell (by Voorhees, Walker, Foley, and Smith).*

FIGURE 1–6. *When AT&T divested itself of the Bell companies in 1984, it also gave up its long-standing bell mark. Bass (now Bass/Yager Associates) created this new mark to reflect the company's global technological scope, which remains today.*

FIGURE 1–7. *The Chase Manhattan Bank logo, created by Chermayeff & Geismar Associates in 1960 (now Chermayeff & Geismar Inc.), shows that even an abstract icon can impart credibility. In fact, the logo has been copied many times in various forms by other financial institutions.*

showed that even an abstract mark can have a profound effect on audience recognition (Figure 1–7).

All these marks are vastly different in their appearance and design approaches, yet they nevertheless have one thing in common: Each aptly and succinctly defines the nature and character of its company. They demonstrate that logo credibility and power can be achieved in numerous ways.

FIGURES 1–8, 1–9. *The facades of these stores leave no question regarding their price points—excellent examples of nonverbal communication.*

1–8

1–9

Nonverbal Communicators

Only about 35 percent of our daily communication experiences are verbal. A whopping 65 percent are nonverbal. *How* something is said is as important as *what* is said. Take a look at the two stores in Figures 1–8 and 1–9. Which would you guess sells more expensive merchandise?

FIGURE 1–10. *The front of this house communicates many things about its inhabitants. They appear to be of modest means, they are neat, and perhaps one of the residents is disabled.*

FIGURE 1–11. *The same is true of this entrance. Obviously, people of wealth reside here—and they don't seem inclined to have many visitors.*

10 •

FIGURES 1–12, 1–13.
*Over 65 percent of our
communication is
accomplished
nonverbally. Gestur-
ing accounts for much
of that.*

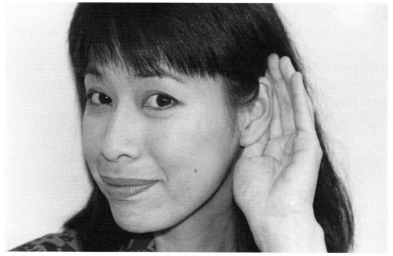

1–12

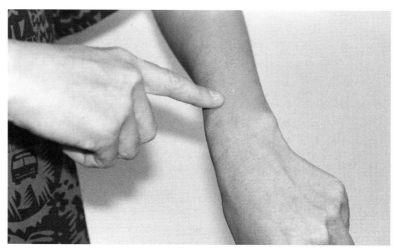

1–13

It's the same with the entrances to the two homes (Figures 1–10
and 1–11). They all are forms of nonverbal communication that we
encounter everyday, everywhere.

Nonverbal communication serves to reinforce, repeat, substi-
tute, complement, accent, regulate—even contradict—verbal
communication. It includes all forms of human communication
that transcends the oral or written word, such as body language
(gesturing, nodding, smiling—Figures 1–12 and 1–13) or visual icons,

FIGURES 1–14, 1–15. Symbols are an integral, powerful part of the communication process. Logos can harness this power to help achieve a company's goals.

1–14   1–15

FIGURE 1–16. The logo proliferates throughout the nonverbal environment.

like the octagonal shape of a stop sign, the palms-up hand of a don't walk sign (Figure 1–14), or the internationally recognized symbols (Figure 1–15) used for a money-exchange center.

Such examples are a reminder that we continually interpret nonverbal cues to help us understand the world in which we live. The same is true of the company logo: It can be the corporate world's most outspoken nonverbal cue. Notice how often the company logo becomes a part of our nonverbal communication environment (Figure 1–16). And notice, too, the different message that logos can send about similar types of companies (Figures 1–17, 1–18, and 1–19).

A **logotype** is the name of a company or product designed in a specific way that is used as a trademark. It is often combined with a symbol, or **mark**, to form a **signature**. In this book, we'll keep it simple by using the more popular terms *logo* or *mark*, rather than

1–17

1–18

FIGURES 1–17, 1–18, 1–19. *Companies in the same type of business can have many different personalities and goals, which can be reflected in a well-designed logo. What does each of these say about its respective network?*

1–19

signature. Yet, astute designers and company leaders know that a logo's mission is anything but simple. A well-designed logo is:

- Both an information vehicle and a persuader.
- A unique mark for that company.
- An embodiment of the essence of a company.
- A visual interpreter of that company's business nature, character, attitude, quality, even its products' price point.
- One that has longevity.
- Credibility-based

Companies both large and small have used logos as essential components in their marketing programs for decades: IBM, Apple, Nike, International Paper, AT&T, CBS, Arm & Hammer—the list goes on and on. Just hearing the names makes most people immediately conjure up images of their symbols, and vice versa. All have logos that are both good-looking and work effectively for them within the context of their respective marketing programs, rather than merely being "likable" or "attractive." They all are embued with **logo power**.

The Elements of Logo Power

How do you achieve logo power? It's a matter of defining the company's character and attributes, discovering what sets it apart from the competition, and determining its goals. Then you must translate all those elements visually into an icon that works to help achieve the company's objectives. Logo power is likewise the product of a symbiotic relationship between graphic designer and client, a process at the heart of which is *total* communication and, therefore, total understanding. Logo power comes about when a logo is designed and implemented in such a way that it:

- Establishes **immediate recognition** for the company.

- Expresses the company's **character or attitude**.

- Conveys the company is an **expert or leader** in its field.

- Instills in the public a sense of **familiarity and trust**.

- Clearly symbolizes, in many instances, the company's line of business.

- In the case of a more abstract mark, is such a **memorable** visual that, when consistently and uniformly applied, becomes a **unique identifier** and, thus, the abstract mark itself takes on meaning and becomes synonymous with the client's business.

- As such, becomes an **endorsement** of that company or organization's product or service.

As an example, look at Prudential (Figure 1–20). What better icon to express reliability, endurance, and strength than the Rock of Gibraltar? And what better attributes would an insurance/financial

FIGURE 1–20. *The Rock of Gibraltar logo has served Prudential well for over a century, projecting perfect attributes for an insurance conglomerate: endurance and stability. The original was created in 1896 by Mortimer Remington, a writer at J. Walter Thompson, for a series of ads. This modernized version was done recently by Prudential's Corporate Identity Department, updating the version created in 1984 by Richard Kontir of Lee & Young Communications. (Reprinted with permission. Prudential and the Rock of Gibraltar logos are registered trademarks of The Prudential Insurance Company of America. All rights reserved.)*

institution want to be known for? Debuting back in 1896, it has undergone 16 transformations over the century to keep it current. Nevertheless, the Rock of Gibraltar, in one form or another, has persevered.

On the other hand, there's Nike. Its abstract, boomerang-shaped "swoosh" (Figure 1–21) doesn't have the inherently stable and immediately recognizable connotations of Prudential's landmark icon. Yet its soaring shape expresses a driving energy—an apt stance for an athletic company. As a result, the "swoosh" emphatically conveys Nike's "in-your-face" attitude of vitality and confidence. These two attributes have been ingrained in the public by every aspect of Nike's world-renowned "Just Do It" marketing campaign, from aggressive ads (Figure 1–22) and its own electrifying Nike Town retail outlets, down to the flamboyant athletes who serve as Nike spokespeople (Figure 1–23).

Few would argue that either of these icons has not been wildly successful in helping establish and maintain a market presence for its respective company. However, that does not mean that the same

FIGURE 1–21. *Nike's curious "swoosh," created in 1971 by Portland State University student Carolyn Davidson, has become one of the most recognized and prolific logos in existence, coming to symbolize the company's in-your-face energy.*

FIGURE 1–22. *The company's aggressive and innovative ad campaigns support Nike's character in every respect.*

FIGURE 1–23. *Some athletes dream of competing in the Olympics; many others dream of being a Nike spokesperson.*

1–24A

Prudential

1–24B

icon would prove a strong image in *any* logo application. To illustrate, try this: Switch the icons so that the Rock of Gibraltar becomes part of Nike's logo (Figure 1–24a–b). Somehow, telling people to "Just Do It," then plastering an inert boulder over the slogan just doesn't do it (unless, of course, you're trying to represent a company that somehow is involved in rock climbing).

The "swoosh" and the Rock only work for Nike and Prudential because, first, each symbolizes what its company's business is all about and, second, it reflects the attitude of that company. As a result, each helps establish the *credibility* of its company. This last point is a vital factor in attaining logo power.

The Power of Credibility

2

IN A NUTSHELL

- One of the most important elements in achieving logo power comes through visually imbuing it with credibility—i.e., making it trustworthy and believable—as long as it truly reflects the client's attitude and business style.

- Credible people and companies are more persuasive than those who are not perceived as such.

- Perception plays a huge role in persuasion, but the best form of persuasion comes when the perception is reality.

- The totally credible company manages its employees by a value system that instills a work ethic leading to excellence in its product and/or service.

- This program of excellence and credibility then can become an outstanding focal point for the company's logo and entire marketing communications plan.

The success of any business or organization lies in its ability to *persuade* its audience to do what it wants, whether that means purchasing a product, using a service, donating money, or whatever. Three elements are associated with persuasion: the communicator's specific disposition or characteristics (**ethos**); the emotional nature of the audience (**pathos**); and the message's features (**logos**). **Rhetoric** is the art of using these elements to effectively persuade.

The ultimate goal of any designer when creating a logo is, of course, to develop a rhetorical and informative mark—one that not only identifies the company and its business, but helps persuade viewers to respond in a specified manner. And one of the most important elements in persuasion (and, thus, achieving logo power) is establishing **credibility**.

Studies in persuation defines *credible* as "expert" and "trustworthy." To be considered credible, a person or company must be seen as both an *expert* in the area the person or company wants to be credible in and as *trustworthy*. Once trust and expertise are established, the person or company can use that credibility to persuade others to respond how they want.

People-to-People Credibility

The credibility principle in interpersonal communication states that a person will be more persuasive if he or she is perceived as credible. The more credible a person is perceived as, the more persuasive he or she will be. People who are considered expert on a subject and who are considered trustworthy will be more persuasive relative to their subject than someone less expert or trustworthy.

To give credibility its proper emphasis, think of television news. Why do you return to a particular station night after night for your daily dose of local and world events? Chances are, it's because of the anchorperson. His or her believability has a huge influence on a network's ratings (and, consequently, on its advertising income). When it comes to world events, who would you believe first—Dan Rather or David Letterman? The trustworthy aspect of such anchors is the main reason many public relations companies strive for what they have determined is the pinnacle of client service—getting a taped PR release aired as legitimate news. They realize the persuasive leverage of the news' *perceived* credibility (i.e., how the public views the news, whether that view is correct or not).

On a more day-to-day level, take Bill Haig's young neighbor Ron. Ron is a whiz with computers. He even has a master's degree in computer science, plus he *looks* the part (Figure 2–1). His beard and dark-rimmed glasses give him a studious air. Then there is Bill's other neighbor, retired master chef Paul (Figure 2–2). He cooks

FIGURES 2–1, 2–2. *Which is the computer whiz and which is the chef? People-to-people credibility persuasion works best when the person not only acts the part, but looks the part, too.*

2–1

2–2

better than anyone Bill knows. Maybe Ron is a great cook and Paul is an expert Net surfer; nevertheless, Bill goes to Paul, not Ron, for restaurant advice, and Ron, not Paul, for computer advice. Each is more credible on subjects related to their particular skills, and each is more credible if they are perceived as experts in those skills.

Perception plays a huge part in persuasion, but the best form of persuasion comes when the *perception* is *reality*. If you represent a company as something it isn't, you can be assured that when the public discovers your deception you're in for a tough—maybe even a useless—battle to reestablish credibility. Remember Charles Keating? He was once a powerful leader in the savings and loan arena, but who would consider him trustworthy today? Many people put their faith in him only to lose their life's savings. Even if Keating truly reformed and repented, in spite of his deep financial knowledge, it is highly unlikely he could ever successfully operate in that industry again.

On the other hand, there's Alan Greenspan, chairman of the Federal Reserve Board. For years he has guided our national economy and, indirectly, that of the entire world. His expertise and trustworthiness are—and must be—above reproach. He is not only *perceived* as credible, he *is* credible.

Company-to-People Credibility

Businesses long ago learned to utilize credibility in persuading consumers. Richard E. Stanley, in his book *Promotion: Advertising, Publicity, Personal Selling, Sales Promotion* (Prentice-Hall, 1982), states:

> Source credibility is a key factor in inducing attitude change through promotional means. A credible, or trustworthy, source produces significantly greater attitude change than one that is not credible. . . . Expertness and trustworthiness are the central requirements for credibility.

FIGURE 2–3. A home-made sign touting fresh eggs for sale is an appropriate marketing tool for this enterprising (if less than artistic) farmer.

FIGURE 2–4. But what does such a sign say about the abilities of this pilot?

He goes on to say that finding a credible leader, or voice, for a company can go a long way in helping sell its product.

Pentagon co-founder Alan Fletcher offers an example that easily puts company-to-person credibility persuasion in perspective. Think of two crude, hand-painted signs (Figures 2–3 and 2–4): one for fresh eggs and the other for flying lessons. The fresh eggs sign is credible because consumers want to think their eggs are produced in a natural "down-home" setting, rather than the mass poultry houses that is likely the case. When you see the hand-done eggs sign, it's easy to imagine the farmer painting it as the hens sit in their nests looking on, all the while happily clucking and popping out fresh eggs. But who would want flying lessons from a company with such a sign? Did the pilots learn to fly from a correspondence course? Did they build their own airplane as well?

Positioning and Credibility

Think back to Ron and Paul, and how each is perceived as an expert in a certain area. That's the way it works when companies want to influence. They use **positioning** to gain their expertise seat, a process that often takes a long time to establish through a carefully formulated and consistently enacted imaging program. As hard as a company's position is to gain, if you're not diligent about maintaining it, those years of work can quickly and easily be lost.

Look at Xerox and IBM as examples. Xerox once tried to enter the computer marketing arena with Xerox Data Systems, but in spite of its leadership position in the copier business, Xerox's computer division failed after only six years. Conversely, IBM made a foray into the copier business, but it too failed. Why? Their expertise was in the one business they were known for, not the other. Both had worked long and hard to position themselves in their respective arenas, then made the mistake of foregoing that position to try something new without careful planning.

Let's take a look at another company that was well known for one thing, but wanted to venture into a new area. Unlike Xerox and IBM, this one managed to do it successfully, using a different approach.

A few years ago, Campbell's decided it would develop a product to take on Ragu spaghetti sauce, but felt that maintaining its strong position in the soup market was paramount. That's why Campbell's chose not to use a marketing technique called **line-extension**, which involves playing off its well-established name. Instead, it wisely distanced its soups from the new product by calling its spaghetti sauces "Prego" rather than "Campbell's Spaghetti Sauce."

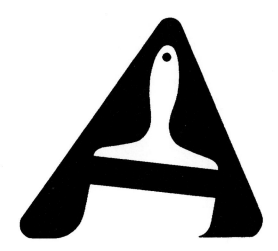

FIGURE 2–5. *A cred-ible logo can convey the expertise of its company by directly relaying the business it is in.*

FIGURE 2–6. *This logo not only conveys the business, but it transmits an emotion-al message of friendliness as well.*

CONTINENTAL

FIGURE 2–7. *When Saul Bass Associates redesigned the Continental Airlines logo in 1968, the airline's credible traits, which the designers wanted to impart in the new logo, were prominently displayed on walls at their workstations.* Given the logo's success, this tactic to keep everyone focused on their goals must have worked.*

One reason Campbell's developed a new name for the sauce is that it realized line-extension names are often overshadowed by the company's original product. Also, in the event Prego failed, Campbell's didn't have to chance that its soup sales might suffer from any negative association.

Luckily, Prego was a major success, and now the company owns two strong names in different lines. (You'll learn more in Chapter 3 about how important a product's name is in positioning it.)

The logo should serve as the credible voice of the company's graphics program. But, once again, just as in the case of a person, the logo must be a believable representation of the business it symbolizes (Figures 2–5 and 2–6) to be effective.

---

* These were: "flight," "high technology," "very progressive/contemporary," "warm-hearted," and "big." Pacifica-Oriental was a sub-theme.

When Saul Bass's firm was redesigning Continental Airlines' logo, Bass kept reminding his staff that Continental's planes did not have to change their logo when flying from airport to airport or country to country. The old Continental mark symbolized "flight" via a contrail form, plus expressed the trustworthy attributes of "high technology," "very progressive/contemporary," "warm-hearted," and "big." These attributes were pinned on every designer's wall in his or her workstation to give direction to the ultimate design. The new logo (Figure 2–7) looked very credible. That's why it worked so successfully from 1968 through the early 1990s, both nationally and internationally.

As the logo designer, it's your job to find out exactly what is at the heart of your client's business operation. By exploring the elements that combine management systems and credibility principles, you can better understand the key elements of a successful company (see Sidebar: "The Totally Credible Company"). Accordingly, you can better judge whether a company plans, develops, and monitors its employees, products/services, and marketing communications to operate as a totally credible company.

Once you understand why credibility is vital to the success of a company, plus why and how that factor can be and should be reflected in the company's logo, you can take this knowledge and apply it to the planning, creation, and implementation of any logo, regardless of the size or nature of the business it will represent.

The Totally Credible Company

A half-century ago James K. Fogleman and others were preaching that for a logo to be effective, it had to accurately reflect the business's attitude and character. In other words, it needed to be designed so as to reflect *credibility*. But the secret of effective credibility persuasion is that the company must not just *look* credible, it must actually *be* credible. Granted, you could develop a logo and image that would probably fool the public for a while. But, eventually, they would catch on and the company, like Charles Keating, may never recoup from the deception.

As humans, we are "value driven." We always act on the basis of our values, whether consciously or subconsciously. Values are of the right sort when they lead one to make the right choices and actions. When these good values are mutually shared within an organization, the resulting harmony ultimately affects management, employees, and the community in positive ways. But a company cannot merely project excellence through visual design, advertising, or public relations without excellence *in reality*.

The totally credible company has not only its own set of good values, but also an excellent product or service, and projects this excellence in all areas of public contact.

In their book *In Search of Excellence*, Tom Peters and Robert Waterman write:

> Every excellent company we studied is clear on what it stands for, and takes the process of value shaping seriously. In fact, we wonder whether it is possible to be an excellent company without clarity on values and without having the right sort of values.

Thus, it follows that the first objective in establishing credibility in the public eye is examining the reality of the company itself. Is it truly an expert in its field? Does it conduct itself in a trustworthy manner? No amount of marketing design will work if the company doesn't know what it is doing or conducts itself incorrectly.

The **totally credible company** maximizes its business expertise and trustworthiness in the way it operates. It manages its employees by a company value system that instills a work ethic leading to excellence in its product or service. Then it communicates this credibility for the purpose of achieving business goals among both its internal public (employees) and external public (customers, investors, and suppliers). This entire program of excellence and credibility can then become an outstanding focal point for the company's marketing communications.

The elements of a totally credible company are:

1. **A statement of goals and objectives.** This establishes in written form what the company wants to accomplish.

2. **An active management-by-values process or total quality management system in place.** This establishes the framework for excellence in the company product or service.

3. **A carefully planned marketing communications system.** This system begins with the company logo, planned with credibility persuasion in mind, then expands to include all visual elements, from stationery and advertising to Web sites.

4. **Continually monitoring and making adjustments.** As the company successfully proceeds through its "life," the company logo will stay intact in its basic "expertise" form, but sustains small adjustments or modifications to maintain "trustworthiness" in its current market atmosphere.

Keeping these elements in mind can help you judge whether the company you are striving to create a credible identity for can actually *be* credible. And they can help you decide whether you want to take on this identity project, or maybe just walk away.

Planning for Power

3

IN A NUTSHELL

- Planning comprises 90 percent of the process of designing a powerful logo.

- A designer often must be willing to act as conflict resolution counselor for a client during the identity development process.

- Having an appropriate name is vital to a logo's success. Instilling credibility starts here.

- You must first accurately define the client's personality and its credibility traits to develop a truly effective logo solution.

- The development of a credibility trait statement involves three steps: the visual audit, stating the company's business objectives, and determining its credibility traits.

- Study the existing logo to gain insight into your client.

- Effective listening and interpretation are key to effective logo planning.

During the course of writing this book, Laurel Harper came across a logo that aptly illustrates how an inappropriate, ill-planned logo can make a negative impression on its public. In a help-wanted ad in a small community newspaper, she spotted a logo consisting of a horse's head inside an omega sign. Presumably, the logo's creator equated the omega with a horseshoe and, thus, finished off the symbol with what he or she must have thought a very clever flourish—the horse.

Now this would have been a perfect logo for something like a horse farm (which were numerous in the area) or a riding stable. However, the business the logo represented was a manufacturer called Omega Plastics. While the logo certainly made a lasting impression, it definitely was not a good one. It left Laurel wondering if plastic is made from horse carcasses.

Where was the *thinking* behind that logo?

In spite of the obvious repercussions of an ill-planned logo, the planning process is often downplayed or, at best, hastily carried out. But consider this: Do architects design a major building without careful planning? Do advertising managers embark on next year's campaign without planning? Do budget directors sign off on next year's company budget without planning?

When Bill was called in to help develop a logo for the City of Honolulu, he had to explain that he is a not a designer, but a design *planner*. He works with the designer like a director works with an actor or actress. And, just as on a movie set, before the creation of any powerful logo can begin there must first be a great script. Painstakingly planning what to say in your logo and how to say it is critical to attaining logo power. In fact, this process is 90 percent of the work involved in developing an effective logo.

That's why most great logos start with a mutually respectful relationship between designer and client. It is of utmost importance that the designer has full respect of management, and vice-versa. In the best-case scenarios, designer/client relationships last many years, and it is of utmost importance that the designer truly understands the company's product or business and its operational attitude before sitting down to develop its logo. That's why the planning process is paramount to a logo's—and ultimately the company's and designer's—success.

Debra Kelley, of Hall Kelley Inc., offers another view on why the planning process is so vital to a successful identity. Her company is often called in to create a new identity program after the client has undergone a major transformation, whether that was the result of a restructuring, merger, change of product line, or whatever. This is where Kelley's interest in organizational development and partner Michael Hall's psychology degree come in handy.

Many times, the transformation leads to internal conflict, anxiety, and pain. "Often the identity development is where that pain is played out," Kelley noted. "People have to face this, come to grips with it, and make decisions about it during the identity development process."

In helping the company redefine itself, Kelley finds she and her staff are not just serving as design consultants; they often act as a sort of conflict-resolution counselor for the company. By helping it come up with a new direction, and in determining the logo needs of the company, the client often is able to clearly define its new direction. And the roles of management and the other employees in helping reach that destination can be articulated. Involving all levels in the planning stages makes everyone more willing to accept and support the final solution, Hall Kelley has found. For this reason alone, the planning process is as crucial to an identity's success as the verbal and visual solutions you devise.

Once you've developed that plan, it is critical that you refer back to it before making any lasting decision about the corporate identity—no matter how tempting it may be to take off in a completely new direction. That's not always easy, especially when you have created a number of attractive logo solutions, but it generally leads to the best choice.

As an example, consider Scott Hull Associate's (SHA) redesign of its logo. SHA is an illustrator's group headquartered in Dayton, Ohio. In 1996, founder Scott Hull wisely recognized that his existing logo (Figure 3–1) no longer reflected the image he wanted his company to project. Plus, it was in need of an update. So he contracted with Siebert Design Associates to redo it.

Hull, a former designer himself, began the process in the right manner by studying his firm's weaknesses and strengths, pinpointing who their existing audience was and who they wanted to add to that group, and by determining where they were and where they wanted to go. He did all the right things. When meeting with the design firm, however, he made a crucial error—he forgot to share *all* his research with them.

FIGURE 3–1. *The redesign of Scott Hull Associate's existing logo demonstrates the importance of paying close attention to your (and/or your client's) research—and to ensuring that everyone involved in the logo design process is made aware of the full scope of these findings.*

Then he almost made a second mistake. Siebert's first logo proposal was fun, quirky, and so attractive (Figure 3–2) that Hull was immediately drawn to it and almost signed off on it. It took a third person—in this case, Laurel Harper—who was a bit removed from the emotional aspect that always accompanies the search for a new identity, but was intimate with Hull's research, to point out that the logo did not fulfill SHA's needs. She, too, thought the proposed solution looked great. But her main concern was that it would not take the illustration group in the direction it was going for two reasons. First, it looked very "Retro." She feared that this design trend had about run its course, so the logo would not catch the attention of the sophisticated design audience SHA wanted to connect with and that it would soon be outdated itself. Second, several parts of the corporate identity campaign Siebert proposed relied heavily on SHA's Midwestern locale. Hull had been working hard to lure New York and West Coast art buyers (a huge segment of the illustration market), and to show that although his office was located in the "down-home Heartland," his illustrators are top-caliber, sophisticated (and nationally located) talents. When Harper pointed this out to Hull, he quickly agreed.

When Lori Siebert was made aware of these concerns—and the full range of the research—she also agreed the proposed solution was not the right one and soon came back with another logo (Figure 3–3). This mark was quirky and fun, yet sophisticated and memorable. It had a look all its own, and definitely embodied what SHA was about and what it wanted to be in the future. In fact, this mark has become the driving force behind the rest of SHA's marketing strategy, inspiring a number of fun, effective campaigns.

FIGURE 3–2. *This proposed solution was so attractive that it almost threw SHA founder Scott Hull off-track. But when he compared it to the needs that he had uncovered in his research, he found that although he liked the logo very much, it did not fulfill those. That is when he also realized that he had forgotten to share all his research with the designer.*

3–3A

3–3B

FIGURE 3–3A AND 3–3B. *Once she was made aware of the full scope of Hull's research, designer Lori Siebert agreed her first proposal was not the right choice. She soon developed another logo that fulfilled all SHA's needs, and now is the basis for the company's entire marketing campaign strategy.*

It All Begins with the Name

First impressions are, we know, often lasting impressions, at least partly because many times a first impression is the *only* opportunity you'll have to make an impact. If you blow it at this stage, chances are you won't get a second shot.

It becomes imperative, then, to make certain that first impression is a good one. In the case of a business, creating a good impression begins with the name, or in many instances the *representation* of that name (your logo). Al Ries and Jack Trout, in their marketing classic, *Positioning: The Battle for Your Mind* (McGraw-Hill, 1981, 1986), remind us that a name is the first point of contact between the message and the mind. Company names communicate verbally the same as company logos communicate visually. Instilling credibility starts here.

A credibility-based name is descriptive of the company business and expresses its expertise factor. Names like Point & Click (Figure 3–4), the Closet Factory, The Travel Network, Mail Boxes Etc., The Bus, Burger King, and Zippy's Fast Food are all good, descriptive, credible names. In contrast, names like Cebit, Retrospex, Plasser American Corporation, Haldex, and Hebasco do not describe the company business, thus negating an opportunity to express their ex-

Point & Click

FIGURE 3–4. *A good name goes a long way in credible logo development. This is an excellent name for a computer training and consulting company. Designer Michael Graziolo simply and succinctly achieves the client's goal of wanting to convey the ease of learning computer technology with his logo solution.*

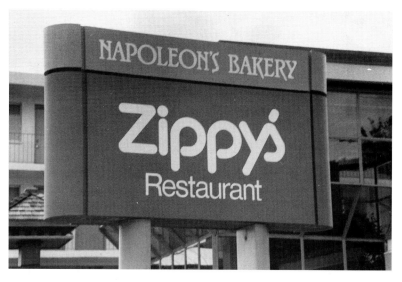

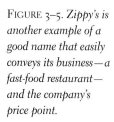

FIGURE 3–5. *Zippy's is another example of a good name that easily conveys its business—a fast-food restaurant—and the company's price point.*

pertise in their respective fields. These names are also difficult to implant in the public mind and, as such, require large marketing investments.

Trustworthy attributes can also be incorporated into a company's name. Names like Compaq (for a compact computer) are not only descriptive, but have trustworthy attributes. With the clever use of the "q" at the end, Compaq suggests "high technology." Names can likewise impart the value of a company or its product. Zippy's, for example (Figure 3–5), suggests "fast," "casual," and "inexpensive," in contrast to something like Le Nouveau Riche Gourmand restaurant, which connotes "formal" and "better check your credit card limit before you come." Compaq and Zippy's are also simple names, easy to communicate and remember. Both are good examples of a credibility-based company name.

Another reason to carefully consider the company name is because it just might establish a subconscious stereotype. In a study described in Ries' and Trout's book, two psychologists were curious about why elementary school students made fun of other classmates who had unusual names. They developed a test in which some fourth- and fifth-grade teachers were unknowingly given a set of fake composition papers to grade, to determine just how far this bias went.

Among the student names assigned to the papers were Hubert, Elmer, David, and Michael. The result? For each group of teachers, the papers bearing the names David and Michael averaged a grade higher than the Huberts and Elmers. Maybe those teachers had watched too many Elmer Fudd cartoons as children?

As a designer, you need to make sure that you don't hang your client with a visual Elmer Fudd. Of course, that's easier to do if the company has a name that is itself imbued with power. That's why many identity designers begin each project by looking at the client's or product's name. In the research phase of its redesign of Federal Express's identity system, Landor Associates found that the word *federal* was no longer serving its company well. When the name was developed in 1973, *federal* gave its company immediate equity, but by the 1990s the word was often associated with *bureaucracy* and *slowness*. On an international level, many people found it hard to pronounce. And, in many parts of Latin America, *federal* was linked with *federales*.

But the shorter version of Federal Express—FedEx—not only was already a popular way many referred to the company, but its fewer letters worked better in various design applications, such as on airplanes and trucks. Along with a tag line, "The World on Time," that clearly expresses the company's key credibility traits, this shortened version became the new public name. Federal Express was retained as the official corporate moniker.

Hornall Anderson Design Works also starts its identity design process by dissecting the origin of the name. Principal Jack Anderson explains that this is critical to how they will graphically interpret it, plus assures they are not just decorating something bad, but are actually building on a great foundation (Figure 3–6). They run each name through a test by determining whether it:

- Sounds good.

- Answers most of the company's objectives.

FIGURE 3–6. *Frappuccino, a combination of* frappe *and* cappuccino, *is just one of the great expressive names in Starbucks Coffee's product line.*

- Follows the "roadmap" the company is traveling along.

- Fits its product mix.

- And, finally, simply feels right.

If the name falls short of meeting these objectives, the design firm encourages the client to get feedback from its own staff and/or client base. This can be done through formal research, focus groups, or "just getting everybody in a room from different corners of the company and agreeing to either buck the system and go with this odd disconnect, or take the time to create a new name," according to Anderson. The point is, if the name doesn't fit right, it will never fit right. "We have done some some pretty amazing things in the past with colors, textures, pretty logos, and all to breathe life into some pretty goofy company names," Anderson added, "but in the end, if it's going to have mileage, the name has to be right."

Another thing Hornall Anderson watches out for are names based on **acronyms/monograms**—those composed of start letters from words making up the company's name, such as IBM (International Business Machines). While IBM itself was a great hit, few have achieved such success since. Anderson likens an acronym/monogram name to an alphabet soup game, where you al-

ways find yourself explaining to clients what the initials stand for.
That's why the design firm steers clients away from this solution and
points them instead in the direction of a short, memorable moniker.

Marketing experts agree that Hornall Anderson is on track when
it says that a name is vital to a company or product's image. In fact,
studies have proven the right name can mean millions of dollars
more in sales over a competitor's product or service. In judging a
company or product name, along with Hornall Anderson's recom-
mendations, other things to consider are:

- Does it begin the positioning process for the client?

- Is it so close to the product description that it can become
  generic, like Lite Beer, from Miller? (This is not so good.)

- Is it close enough that it is almost generic, like People magazine? (This is good.)

- Will it have longevity, or is it based on a trend that may be short-
  lived and, thus, quickly make the name outdated or obsolete?

Aside from coming up with a name that could possibly be more
workable in the logo design, once a client has gone through the
process of scrutinizing its name, no matter what the outcome (even if
it's not what you'd like it to be), the process is likely to lead to a total
buy-in by your client regarding building that name's image. Plus,
during this course of study, tangible attributes that need to be inter-
preted graphically in the logo are inevitably brought to the surface.

Jack Anderson cautions designers to not make changes for
change's sake. If the existing name has heavy equity, it should stay.
The last thing you want to do is throw out years of consumer recognition.

Once the name is set in stone, Hornall Anderson looks at its
components to determine what its equity is—which segment of the
name has the most or an inherent interest to it—then proceeds from
there with its identity design.

Developing the Credibility Trait Statement

When Saul Bass & Associates designed the Rockwell International logo (Figure 3–7), a task force made up of the client's top management gave the firm 14 business goals to achieve. Using these goals as its guide, the design team's first step was to determine the credibility attributes the Rockwell logo should incorporate to achieve them. The designers' thinking was that Rockwell's logo (in fact, its entire communications system) should be planned to express the company's unique credibility attributes. Not all designers are lucky enough to have a client like Rockwell who already knows what it wants its logo to achieve. In such cases (which is most of them) it's up to you as the designer to help your client decipher this conundrum.

To be of value, the logo must contribute to achieving the client's business objectives. This means that you must determine what business objectives your client wants to achieve and what credibility traits will get it there. A **credibility trait statement** can help you do this. Having a carefully defined (and approved) credibility trait statement has an added benefit: When you present your proposed solution, your client can judge it on the basis of whether the

FIGURE 3–7. *Saul Bass Associates was given over 14 business goals by Rockwell International's management that the client wanted to achieve with its new logo. While not all designers are lucky enough to have such a well-informed client, by carefully researching your project you can help your client define its goals.*

logo you have created visually expresses what was defined in the credibility statement. You have something in writing that provides you with a solid argument for your solution (provided you followed the statement's objectives).

The end result, then, is not just what you or someone else might like. It is something that can be judged based on whether it communicates those established credibility criteria.

Three steps can help you develop your client's credibility trait statement:

1. A visual audit.
2. Stating the company's business objectives.
3. Defining its credibility traits.

Step 1: *The Visual Audit*

Remember that looking credible means all areas of public contact must be utilized to develop a powerful marketing communications system. This requires a visual audit of all areas of the company's public contact, both external and internal.

Start by taking all your client's existing printed pieces, from stationery and business cards to forms and brochures, and sticking them on a wall in appropriate categories. Then photograph all elements of the image program that you can't physically put up on this wall, such as company vehicles, product packaging, company clothing, or signage. Put their photos on the wall, also in the correct categories. In short, if the company name goes on it, place it on the wall. Your objective is to view how areas of public contact are currently working together (or not working) as a unified communication system. Do the same with your client's competitor's logo applications.

A typical company will look like a dozen or so different businesses using the same name. Your objective is to make it look like one company with appropriate credibility attributes communicating as a singular system.

Step 2: State Your Client's Business Objectives

The next step is to question your client about what its business goals will be one, five, maybe as far off as ten years from now. Then write them down. This is what your new marketing communication system is to achieve.

A word of caution: It's important that the client be specific. If the client responds "increase sales," you must get the client to pin it down much more, such as "expand to the West Side market" or "double the number of seniors using my product." So keep asking until you get to the nitty-gritty.

As an example, some objectives that might be important include:

- *Attracting top-caliber employees and reducing turnover.* Railings, Inc., was in the business of installing freeway railings and signs. All its work was for the State of Hawaii Highway Department, consistently bidding against one competitor. Low bid always got the job. How did Railings stay competitive? Company president Ray Wulfert did everything possible to attract the best workers and reduce turnover, so work was done at a lower cost even though its salaries were higher than its competitor's. One of the ways it attracted and kept its employees was through a well-planned logo design program. A credible logo was at the heart of Railings, Inc.'s marketing communications system. It was employed on trucks, T-shirts, hard hats, and so on. Employees felt a part of the company, part of the successful system of excellence in everything Railings did.

- *Better supplier relations.* Most companies purchase products for their business, making supplier relations an important objective. Satisfied vendors might just help keep a company's prices competitive, as they will be more likely to offer it their best prices, make deliveries on time, and provide it with top-quality products. As such, good supplier relations might just give your client a competitive edge.

- *Increasing financial (including shareholder) relations.* Unless it's as wealthy as Bill Gates or the Sultan of Brunei, how bank-ers, stock analysts, and others in the financial community view a company will probably be very important to its business some-day. You never know when a quick infusion of cash to get over a hump may be needed.

- *An ability to move into new markets.* In the late 1960s before deregulation, Continental Airlines was seeking to expand into the Pacific—first to Hawaii and then across to the Orient. One of its major objectives was to look Pacifica/Oriental. Remember the shell-like "flight" logo in red on the golden tail? It also was a flight symbol. Other trustworthy elements include looking tech-nological (airlines should look technological, not cutesy, for fear-of-flying reasons) and big (for the same reasons).

In another example, the Hawaii-based fast food chain Zippy's had a long-time following of the local Japanese, Chinese, Por-tuguese, and Filipino market, but the growth market in Hawaii was Westerners. So, its logo (Figure 3–8) was redesigned to look more "mainland" in an attempt to appeal to this group. Market expansion

FIGURE 3–8. *Zippy's old logo had become too "local" in appearance for the new market the Hawaii-based fast-food restaurant wanted to appeal to—Westerners.*

FIGURE 3–9. *The new logo looks much more "mainland."*

and sales took off after the new logo (Figure 3–9), food items, and architectural changes were implemented.

How do you determine what a company wants to achieve in the near and long term? Do all of the following:

1. Talk not just to management, but staff throughout the company in other departments or divisions.

2. Study your client's competition. Do a visual audit of the logos. What are the business goals? What are the strengths and weaknesses in accomplishing these goals?

3. What are the trends for companies in your client's field?

Step 3: Define Your Client

This important step determines the design criteria used as the basis for planning the look of your client's new credibility-based logo and subsequent marketing communications system. Remember that credibility has two major prongs: expertise and trustworthiness. Your client's business should define its expertise factor, providing it is truly an expert at it. If you are designing a logo for a painting contractor, photographer, or pool mechanic, this step is easy. At the extreme might be a multifaceted company like Rockwell International. (Saul Bass defined it as being in the "high technology" business.)

Defining the trustworthy factor of credibility is a little harder, but not that much. Start by asking your client what personality it should have, as if the company were a person (see Sidebar: "A Client-Defining Questionnaire"). For instance, a bank might want others to think of it as "stable, secure, professional, and easy to do business with," while an airline might want to be regarded as "highly technological, efficient, safe, and big, yet friendly." An amusement park would want to be viewed as "fun and exciting," while a city public transit system would probably favor "professional and friendly." The trick is to get the client to place itself in its important public's shoes and define itself as they (the public) see it. It's really what the public considers to be your client's important trustworthy attributes that counts.

To find out how your client's public actually does view it, survey customers, vendors, business partners, etc. It may be interesting to learn just how much your client knows about its public image.

Also, go through some pieces written about the company, such as speeches, advertisements, company profiles, and press releases. When you come to an attribute, write it down (see Table 3–1: *An Attribute List*). Write it down again when it appears again. When you've finished, tally up how many times each attribute appears. This is a form of content analysis, a professional research methodology.

Pin Down the Personality

If you don't think defining your company's personality and internal culture is important, take a look at what happened to Arizona Public Service (APS). In 1994, this Phoenix-based utilities company produced a booklet on ethical standards for its employees. The logo it selected for the book showed two people pointing at a star. Ironically, some employees decided the logo closely resembled a satanic

A Partial List of Trustworthy Attributes

TABLE 3-1

Refer to the attribute list often in this table. This is just a starter set. You'll probably have more to add. Not all attributes are important, only the richest in value or importance to your client's particular business endeavor. Some attributes will combine automatically with others, such as "profitable" and "productive."

Secure	Pragmatic
Modern	Exciting
Integrity	Established
Large	Reliable
Productive	Quality-minded
Conservative	Competitive
Progressive	Flexible
Responsible	Dedicated
Technological	Responsive
Committed	Proactive
Energetic	Traditional
Trendy	Stable
Innovative	Admired
Prominent	Orderly
Cutting-edge	Old-fashioned basics
Dedicated	Futuristic
Unique	Dynamic

symbol, and refused to read the book on ethics. This was after months had been spent reviewing it, and 10,000 copies had been distributed to 25 different locations. In the end, APS decided that rather than throw out the time and effort that had been spent producing the booklet, it would verbally describe its policies to anyone who would not read them. "No matter how hard you work to do things right, there is an importance of knowing the culture within your company," one APS manager, in hindsight, told the news media.

Of course, there are many ways that enterprising designers decipher their clients' personalities to develop the design platform. For instance, Hornall Anderson assembles what it calls an "attitude board." These are 16-x-20-inch collages, of color, typefaces, textures, and photographs, designed to elicit reactions on tone and mood from the client and/or its audiences (Figures 3–10 and 3–11). What goes on the boards is determined by the parameters of the client's project. Based on how the client reacts to the boards, the firm gets a feel for its personality. In fact, the attitude board has proven so successful that Hornall Anderson uses this technique for clients who have existing graphics programs as well as those who don't.

Study the Existing Logo

Not all logo designs are going to start from scratch. Often, you are updating an existing one. If this is the case with your project, you can use the old logo to help you further define who and what your client is or wants to be. You should study the old logo to see how it meets—or fails to meet—your client's current goals.

Changing a logo can be an intense, expensive process—much more so than developing an identity for a new company. Still, many circumstances justify creating a new logo or modifying the existing one, especially when the change is used to signal that something important has happened to the company. Such instances might include (more than one may apply):

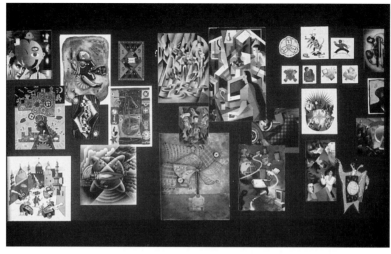

3–10

FIGURES 3–10, 3–11.
Hornall Anderson Design Works creates "attitude boards" to show its clients in the early stages of researching an identity project. These help it to define the client's personality and credibility traits, plus discern its design likes and dislikes.

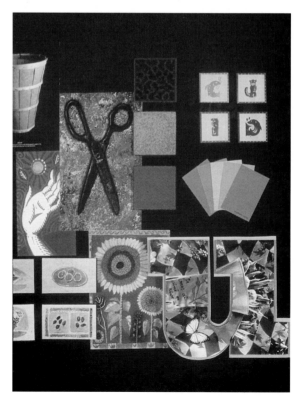

3–11

1. Key management has been replaced, or there is a new owner. In the case of such an internal change, your client might need to heighten employee relations, financial confidence, government relations, customer relations, or supplier relations.

2. The nature of your client's business has changed.

3. Or, possibly, the nature of its business has become clearer. For instance, the company sold off divisions or product lines that didn't fit its main business.

4. It needs to communicate clearly, with one voice, in a business climate of highly competitive marketing communication.

5. Company subsidiaries need to associate directly with the parent logo or disassociate, adopting separate logos on their own.

6. Two companies have merged to form one.

7. Two companies have merged, and in the process are forming a new business basis.

8. The company business strategy changed or was newly defined.

9. The company communication strategy has changed or been re-defined.

10. Your client's competition has become more competitive.

11. Your client desires to develop a broad awareness of its personality, its sense of values and, as such, wants to become known as more "personal."

12. Your client needs to communicate a "look" consistent with how it conducts itself in reality. For example, if it has become more "progressive" it needs to look like it.

13. It wants to attract or retain quality employees.

14. It needs to organize a subsidiary structure and company names, for future growth.

15. Your client wants to show leadership in a crowded business field.

16. Your well-established client needs to clearly reflect the continuity of its achievements in the past and its promises for the future.

17. It needs to reflect cohesion and a sense of purpose in all areas of public contact.

18. Your client needs to position itself in a niche market, product, or service line.

19. It needs to support a superior product or service with appropriately superior graphic design.

Taking the time to determine why your client is changing its logo can not only help you form the basis for your design solution, but can also give you insight into the client's wants and needs.

Did I Say That?!

How often have you been misunderstood when you thought you were stating your case clearly, or have you misunderstood someone else? And how often has this resulted in conflict? There's no doubt that, although we may speak the same language, the way that language is translated can be as varied as our sexes, upbringing, regional differences, etc. It's important then, when working with a client, to determine its goals, attitudes, and perceptions, so that what you *heard* they wanted is not only what you give them, but it actually *is* what they wanted.

That's not easy. Effective communication is distorted by many barriers, including the following.

- **Selective listening.** We often hear only what we want to hear or expect to hear, and screen out everything else.

- **Evaluating the credibility of the source.** Refer again to the earlier discussion regarding Dan Rather and David Letterman on page 21.

- **Differences in perceptions.** Have you heard the story about the boy who, after a baseball game, questioned the umpires about how they call balls and strikes? The first replied, "Well, some's balls, and some's strikes, and I calls 'em as I sees 'em." The second umpire said, "Well, some's balls and some's strikes, and I calls 'em as they are." And the third said, "Well, some's balls and some's strikes, but they ain't nothin' till I calls 'em." We don't learn so much about America's great pastime from this as we do about how people are all different. And those differences are going to lead to many perceptions of the same thing.

- **Nonverbal cues.** There was a great skit on *Saturday Night Live* in which Jane Curtin hosted a talk show based on sarcasm. Her every question and remark was punctuated with nonverbal gestures that belied the sweet talk she was making with her guest— things such as, "You were just *wonderful* in that last movie you starred in," all the while rolling her eyes into her head. The skit was a classic example of how words can mean just the opposite of what you're saying if the body language works in opposition to the verbal language. You must always be on the alert for *how* a client says something as well as *what* they say.

These are just a few ways in which clear communication can be thrown off track.

At the least, you can somewhat circumvent any misinterpretation by always repeating back to your client what you *think* they said. Hall Kelley, however, has come up with something much better. It developed a system several years ago called the Chair Test to ensure that it clearly understands the client. Granted, it's a little unusual. Nevertheless, clients find it entertaining and, even better, it gets great results and serves as an early warning system in the design process.

It works like this: During the preliminary stages of an identity

3–12

3–13

3–14

FIGURES 3–12, 3–13, 3–14. *Hall Kelley Inc. uses what it calls the "Chair Test" to define its clients personalities, and ensure they are all speaking the same language. The design firm gathers key decisionmakers in the client's identity process and shows them slides of chairs, to which the client participants attach descriptive attributes. Hall Kelley Inc. then narrows down exactly what that description means to the participants. For instance, if a client says it wants a chair in its office that shows it is on the "leading edge," they are shown slides of chairs until they find one that matches their perception of "leading edge." This clues Hall Kelley Inc. in to how far that client is willing to go to achieve a "leading edge" look with its identity.*

project, they gather the client's key participants in the process and Debra Kelley shows them slides of different types of chairs (Figures 3–12, 3–13, and 3-14). The participants are then asked to attach descriptive attributes to each. Based on their answers, the design firm can decipher exactly what the client means when it tells them it wants something like, "We're leading edge." Kelley keeps showing them examples of chairs until the participants select one that, in their perception, accurately represents "leading edge." Using the answers as a guide, Hall Kelley can then establish an aesthetic benchmark from which to develop a design program, based on the client's perceptions of itself—whether the client recognized that was how it saw itself or not.

The Final Platform

Once you have determined the credibility factors and the client's personality, you can use them to compile your design platform (design criteria or design brief), which is a written statement of what you are striving for with the client's identity program. This can then become an invaluable guide for you during the design process, something you can refer to time and again to keep focused.

You can use all of the steps outlined here, a combination of them, or create your own (following these as a guide) to develop a research methodology you and the types of clients you usually work for might be comfortable with. But no matter which path you choose to follow, you are still bound for the same destination: In the end, you want to be able to compile a concise statement of who your client is in terms of credibility persuasion—that is, a summation of its expertise and trustworthy factors—which defines how the company wants to be known. A truly creative credibility-based logo design will then express these traits dynamically.

A Client-Defining Questionnaire

The following client questionnaire, developed by Malcolm Grear Designers, can help define your client's expertise and trustworthy factors. (Several design firms use a similar survey.) In each instance, you should adapt the wording to fit your client's business, but don't alter the *intent* of the questionnaire. It asks the right questions to elicit the right answers. Malcolm Grear Designers uses it as a tool to provide information on how the best solution for the design problem might be achieved. Additionally, it leads clients into conversations regarding what their companies are all about. This ultimately helps define their personalities, in combination with the answers.

1. How would your describe your company/business to someone who has no knowledge of its existence?

2. Does this description accurately reflect how you would like to be known?

3. What is the strategic mission for (client name)?

4. What are the short-term goals/plans? Long-term?

5. What are your dreams for (client name)?

6. What do you see as obstacles to those achievements?

7. What are your greatest strengths/attributes?

8. What are your greatest weaknesses?

9. How do you think the public perceives you?

10. What will (client name) likely be in ten years?

11. How do you differentiate (client name) from your competitors?

12. Define the audience that is most important to you in terms of conveying a distinct visual image.

13. What is your current visual image?

14. In your opinion, is this image recognized?

15. Describe one visual that would appropriately represent (client name).

16. Is there anything else?

In addition to Malcolm Grear Designers' questions, you might add the following:

17. Customers might describe your company differently than company managers. What is the difference, if any, between their version(s) and the managers'?

18. What do you want to achieve with your new logo?

19. Some internal publics and external publics may say that a new logo is not necessary. If so, what are their main arguments?

20. Some may say a new logo is absolutely necessary. What are their main arguments?

The Design Process

4

IN A NUTSHELL

- Most logos are one of three types: acronyms/monograms, name only, or name/symbol combinations.

- When selecting type, color, shapes, pictorial icons, and the other components of your design, you must consider not just what looks good, but what conveys your client's credibility traits, too, for the logo to have true power.

- Credibility can be visually articulated in a number of ways, from metaphorical icons to those that directly represent the type of business your client is in—even through how the company name and symbol are juxtaposed.

- Don't try to pack too many credibility traits into the logo. Limit it to the most important.

- A good rule of thumb to follow in all aspects of logo design is to keep it simple.

The planning process is complete. The design objectives are clear to both you and your client. The design brief is written, also clear to all. Now it's time to get going on the actual design.

The Three *Ls*

Before you get into designing logos based on credibility persuasion, you must first understand the basics of logo design. Most company logos are of three types (though there are several variations on these).

Acronyms or Monograms

As the name suggests, these are made up of the first letters of each word in the company name, such as Owens-Illinois (Figure 4–1). While this sounds like an easy way out, remember Jack Anderson's word of caution: Don't get into this method of identification unless your client is prepared to spend a lot of money to establish it. Companies like IBM have done exactly that. Small businesses cannot afford to, nor is it necessary, since pairing the company name

FIGURE 4–1. *O-I (Owens-Illinois) is an example of a monogram logo. Notice how the treatment of the letters almost forms an abstract symbol.*

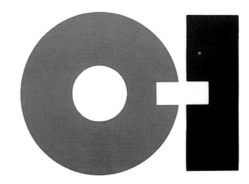

with a symbol is a much better way to convey credibility. Acronym
logos are also difficult to design to impart credibility attributes, as
the letters limit what can be done with the shape. Too little design
says nothing, too much becomes confusing. Here's an example:

> The Electric Transit Vehicle Institute once tried to establish an
> ETVI acronym logo. Instead, it discovered it was losing the exper-
> tise factor (electric transit vehicle) inherent in its name. Finally, a
> simple logo symbolizing electric transit vehicle technology replaced
> the acronym. The result was a positive credibility and marketing
> communications impact. Learn from ETVI's error and, unless let-
> ters really are your name (e.g., ABC Convenience Store), stay away
> from acronyms and monograms.

Name-Only Logos

Company name logos such as Xerox (Figure 4–2) and the current Mobil logo (Figure 4–3) are a one-step communication tool;
the logo *is* the name. Their advantage is that there are no symbols
consumers must learn to relate with the names. The downside is

4–2

4–3

*FIGURES 4–2, 4–3.
Two widely recognized
name-only logos.
While over the years
there has been some
disagreement as to
whether the nostalgic
Pegasus symbol
(adopted in 1911)
should remain part of
Mobil's logo, the
name-only version has
prevailed.*

that names are very difficult to design to impart credibility attributes. A name does not often connote the expertise factor (i.e., the company business). They are usually designed within a shape, which also can inhibit communicating the company business and trustworthy attributes.

Name/Symbol Combination

This is generally the best logo design for several reasons: It provides an easy way to convey the business your company is in via the symbol, plus the symbol's design can also impart your trustworthy attributes (Figure 4–4).

Credibility and Aesthetics

You already know the basic design components of the logo, and certainly you're an expert at working with type, color, and shape, and fashioning harmonious, attractive layouts. But to create the credibility-based, powerful logo what you now must do is apply your design

FIGURE 4–4.
A name/symbol combination.

**Southdale
Pet Hospital**

FIGURE 4–5. *Type alone can impart many attributes.*

Greater First National Bank of Bedford

Greater First National Bank of Bedford

skills in an aesthetically pleasing manner, all while carefully considering how you can use each logo element to convey the the client's credibility attributes and personality traits. Just a few considerations you must deal with are:

Type

There is no end to the choice of typefaces from which to choose today and, of course, the computer makes it easy to create an entirely unique font for your client. Still, you must judge your choice on not just which face will look good, but which is sensitive to your client's needs. Contemporary Brush condensed might be a great choice for a café with its lighthearted, energetic appeal, but what kind of message would it send out if your client is a financial institution (Figure 4–5, top)? You will want to stick with a more traditional choice, like Times New Roman bold (Figure 4–5, bottom). And don't forget that type style can impact how the logotype is perceived. Bold, italics, condensed, extended, etc.—they all convey inherent emotional as well as visual messages. And, of course, in the case of a name/symbol combo, you want to spec a typeface that complements the symbol. So it's not just a matter of sitting down with your favorite type house catalog and selecting the font *de jour*, or booting up your font development program to create something totally wild or different. You must carefully weigh how that type choice is going to help or detract from your client achieving its marketing goals, both now and in the future. A final word of caution, however. Keep the typeface simple when combining with the company symbol. Let the symbol carry the communication load. The company name in a typeface should supplement quietly.

Color

It's the same with color. The right color can dramatically increase (or decrease) the power of a logo. You would not use lilac for a car repair shop, for example, but it might be a good choice for a beauty salon or a new perfume. Burgundy or royal blue connote stability and authority; primary colors are perfect for children's products; earthtones send out a message of environmental friendship; and so on. You must also consider what color(s) your client's major competitors use. You want to ensure that viewers don't become confused as to which company's or product's logo they're viewing, so you will likely want to refrain from choosing a hue that is closely associated with another company's logo, especially one operating in the same marketing arena. And, of course, you need to consider how your logo will look in black and white, as inevitably it will be used this way in many circumstances. If the logo does not work in black and white, it will never work any better in color.

Other considerations when speccing color include budget. When your client has a lot of money, it is possible to do almost anything in color: multiple colors, bleeds, etc. However, in most cases, such a budget is not going to be available, and your client will greatly appreciate prudence on your part. In fact, even the well-financed companies don't mind a savings now and then. When Landor Associates redesigned Federal Express's identity in 1992, the company was very pleased over the nearly $10 million in labor and materials it saved when the new logo design eliminated the purple field from the company's 10,000 tractor trailers. So, unless you've discussed this in advance and your client has told you "no holds barred," keep it as simple as possible — it prevents problems down the road. And remember: Some of the most successful identity systems, like AT&T, Nike, and "Big Blue" (IBM), use single-color trademarks.

Don't overlook the reproducibility of the color palette you select. You may work in an area where you have access to one of the
best printers in the world, a printer that can perform miracles with
all your complex design requests and color matches, but will your
client? Sticking with Pantone Matching System® colors that every
printer is going to be familiar with and have readily available is a
smart choice. Also, if your color speccing gets too complicated, how
likely is this to create a registration problem? Embossing problem?
Die-cut problem?

Shapes

Circles or squares; curves or straight lines; bold rules or delicate
underscores; precise, machine-set lines or brushstrokes—all will affect the way your logo is perceived, as well as how it reproduces. Additionally, it will affect the formats for future usage, such as whether
it will work on a vertical or horizontal sign or banner.

To make matters even more complicated, you can't just limit
your thinking to the actual look of your logo. You must also consider
its implementation requirements.

Implementation

Your logo must be capable of working on everything from a
matchbook or an embossed business card to the side of a building or
a billboard (Figure 4–6). And you'll probably have to second-guess
your client on just how it will be used in the future. As his or her
business grows and diversifies, so will the uses for its logo increase. It
is likely to be far more widely used than originally envisioned. It's
up to you to be the soothsayer.

As a quick checklist, here are some functional considerations to
keep in mind:

1. Will the logo adapt to present and future applications, such as
   vehicles, signage, uniforms, and so on?

2. Will it adapt to CD, electronic, laser, and dot matrix reproduction?

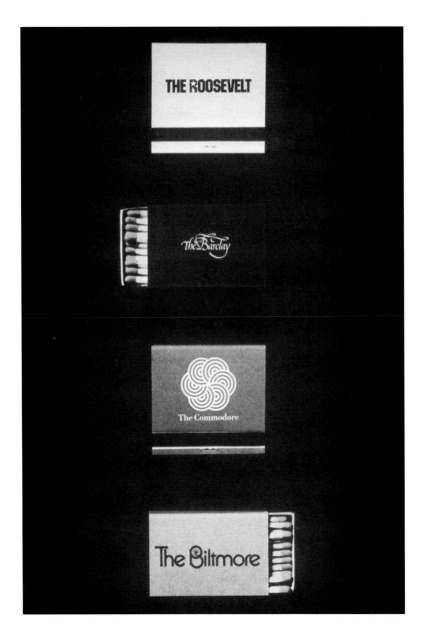

FIGURE 4–6. *An ability to "read" well in various sizes is vital to a logo's effectiveness. While the logos shown here work well on these matchbook covers, they must also adorn the sides of buildings.*

3. Will it reproduce on a variety of materials?

4. Will it communicate at every distance, whether short-range or long-range?

5. Will it reproduce in black and white, and in color? Is registration critical? If so, is your client truly capable of ensuring that its integrity will be maintained in all printing applications?

Flexibility

Who knows how many products or divisions your client may end up with? Your client will surely appreciate you more if your logo (or a slightly modified variation of it) can carry through the company identity in various usages. (Of course, if you think your logo may end up adorning a product, such as a T-shirt, that is going to be sold for profit, you might want to negotiate a royalty arrangement.)

Internationally Understandable and Acceptable

If you know that your client will be using your design on an international basis, you want to proceed very carefully. You should make certain that your design can be understood across language barriers (a symbol might work best) and that the symbol and colors you choose are acceptable in all cultures.

Longevity

Many business owners and designers today think a logo needs to last only five years or so. Once again, you need to second-guess your client. While there may, indeed, be circumstances where the logo does not need to endure (such as a one-shot fundraiser, for example), it takes a long time to build consumer recognition. So why not go for a winner from the onset? Of course, creating a mark with longevity can be one of the hardest aspects of identity design. Look at Procter & Gamble's man-in-the-moon mark. After a hundred years, it had to be virtually abandoned because, of all things, some viewers decided it had a satanic aspect to it. Who can predict why some logos will stand the test of time, while others fail? One thing you can watch out for, however, is creating a mark that is based too heavily on current trends. You can almost be certain that these will have a very short life.

On the Mark

The next step is to actually begin developing a set of visual examples that might be appropriate solutions (Figure 4–7). Start your design by studying the name of the business or product you are designing for. (Of course, you already know it is *the* perfect name, as you covered this base in the planning stage.) What is it about the name that stands out? Is it an interesting spelling that you could play up typographically? Does it evoke strong imagery? Maybe it has an interesting sound to it. Or is there another aspect of the company that might work better, such as the very nature of the business (Figure 4–8)?

Then, if your client has an existing logo, study it. Strip it down to to its basics and scrutinize each part to understand what went on with it before you got to it. What was good about it? What was bad? What should be kept? What should not? Just as with the company's name, you need to establish how much equity was in the existing logo. Does it still reflect what its company is all about? Is it truly an inappropriate or bad icon, or does it simply need a little updating, retaining its key visual elements, to bring it into the present? For instance, looking at Federal Express again. In the course of researching its new design, Landor found that the colors of the old logo—purple and orange—were very powerful in communicating urgency and leadership. So they retained those in the new version, pumping them up even more by adding red to the purple and subtracting it from the orange to achieve greater visibility and vitality. This had the added benefit of minimizing the old colors' tendency to appear blue and red when poorly reproduced.

Remember: A lot of time and effort goes into establishing pub-

FIGURE 4–7. *This ex-*
ample of his design
thought process
demonstrates how the
late Saul Bass achiev-
so many memorable
gos in his long and
ellar career.

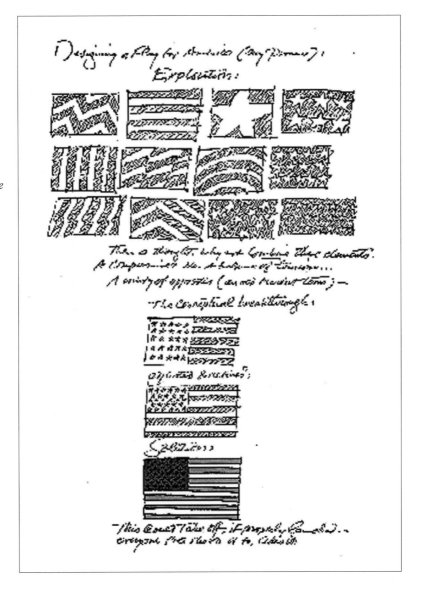

FIGURE 4–8. *The obvious approach is often the best, especially when it comes to conveying the nature of your client's business. Still, as this example shows, the obvious can also be very interesting and aesthetically appealing.*

lic recognition for a logo, so you don't want to undo years of effort based only on the fact that the existing symbol is not the way *you* would have done it. This is when you need to set all ego aside, step back, and judge it fairly.

Now look again at the attribute list you developed for your client. You need to think about how to convey these features in the new logo, and which should be emphasized. One of the best rules to follow is: Simplicity—generally—is the best way. No matter how many attributes you uncovered about your client during the credibility trait statement research, don't try to pack too many of them into one symbol. Only the most important, or richest, traits need be developed.

That's not always easy. If your client is a global communications firm, you might be tempted to incorporate technology, the international aspect, and speed of communications into your design. Yet this could be telling too much of a story. The logo may become too complex. Some of the company story can be told through other outlets (maybe advertising) or perhaps some of the story is something

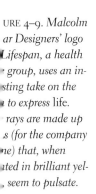

URE 4–9. *Malcolm*
ar Designers' logo
Lifespan, a health
group, uses an in-
sting take on the
to express life.
rays are made up
s (for the company
ne) that, when
ated in brilliant yel-
, seem to pulsate.

that will automatically be assumed by the public anyway. High-tech
communications is *supposed* to be fast, so this attribute may not
even need to be pointed out. Jack Anderson admits this has happened to him before and it took an astute client to point out that he
was striving for too much. That is why he advises all designers to listen to their clients and make sure the design process involves a
hand-in-glove relationship with that client.

Once you know which trait(s) you want to convey, how will you
do it? Is it a matter of incorporating a metaphorical icon into the
logo that will connote that attribute, such as an oak tree for strength
or the sun for life (Figure 4–9)? Or perhaps you will use a direct
symbol representation of the client's business (Figures 4–10 and
4–11). Even the way you position the symbol with the name, in the
case of a name/symbol logo, can affect how that logo and your
client are perceived (Figure 4–12). Study the samples in Chapter 6
to learn more about how a logo can be creatively and attractively
imbued with credibility traits.

FIGURES 4–10, 4–11. *It's very easy to distin-guish the nature of the businesses these two logos represent. The stylized building in 4–10 is easily recog-nized, while in 4–11 the circular shape and wavy line combine to represent a CD and rhythm, readily sym-bolizing this Japanese recording company.*

4–10

4–11

FIGURE 4–12. *How the name and symbol are juxtaposed in name/symbol logos can affect the message. The top version connotes "strong and credible," while the other three have a more contemporary feel. In practicality, various demands and applications, such as the layout of an ad or letterhead, or that of a horizontal truck or vertical banner, often result in the use of several variations.*

It's Judgment Day!

You've concluded the logo development phase. Now you must present the final solution to your client. In some cases, you may have more than one choice to offer. It's your job to help your client determine the best logo from what may appear to be an equally deserving lineup. How?

The first step is to review the objectives and design criteria agreed upon at the beginning of the assignment. Everyone in the room should reacquaint themselves with the credibility attributes established in the planning stage. The final logo design should stand on the basis of meeting the objectives and criteria of the assignment. The question is not, "Do you like it?" It is only, *"Does it meet criteria?"* Then, and only then, will you truly have a solution to a predefined, credibility-based logo. As important, it gives objectivity to the final solution, which allows for an easy decision. Verbal design criteria equals final design solution. That's it.

If your client doesn't feel these criteria have been met or all functional aspects accounted for in the options presented, ask him or her to outline what each lacks and, if necessary, you must try again. More often than not, it will take weeks of intense effort to find that perfect solution (although you shouldn't discount the possibility of a first hit). So don't try to rush the process.

Don't be concerned if you must go back to the drawing board a second or even a third time before you and your client are happy. If the planning and design development work was done properly, you should eventually find a mutually agreeable solution. With an understanding of the planning process based upon credibility persuasion, both of you will have the ability to judge the best logo alternative.

Is Your Logo Legal?

It's happened more than once, even to some of the most-respected design firms. You develop what you think is a unique logotype for your client, only to have it contested by another company for looking too much like its own mark. If found negligent, your client could be out a lot of money compensating the original owner for trademark **infringement**, even if it was an innocent mistake. Your logo doesn't have to be a replica of the other company's in order to be declared an infringement, and even if the courts rule in your favor, you and/or your client will probably be out a lot of money defending your design.

So, what determines when your design is too close to another's? Normally, likelihood of confusion is the main issue; that is, how much chance is there that a viewer will think your logo is actually the other company's?

With the vast number of logos registered today in the United States alone, and with certain industries having icons that are specific to them and, thus, often natural choices for incorporating into their logo designs, it's not always easy to develop a signature that is guaranteed to be free from infringement. Some businesses specialize in researching your logo options to make sure there are no others out there that look like yours. Still, accidents do happen and you might find yourself in a lawsuit.

How do the courts determine whether you infringed on the other company's mark? In 1973, the U.S. Supreme Court made a ruling that can be used to judge if a logo would result in the "likelihood of confusion." It established nine items to consider in trademark infringement cases:

1. Similarity of the two companies' goods and services. This is the key litmus test.

2. Similarity of trade channels.

3. The length of time the logos were used without confusion.

4. Similarity of the appearance and sound of the logos.

5. Amount of actual confusion.

6. The number and nature of similar marks on the market.

7. Type of sale: whether it was an impulse or considered purchase.

8. Similarity of trade channels.

9. The variety of goods that have the logos.

The authors are not legal consultants, however, keep these things in mind when designing your mark to protect yourself from a lawsuit. And, at the same time, strive for a logo design that will be easy for your client to protect from any others infringing on it. If you have any doubts about the mark you are creating, certainly invest in the time and expense to have it thoroughly researched and/or consult a lawyer (preferably a trademark specialist). Such upfront cost is likely to be a lot less expensive than the price you'll pay to defend your design. Plus, the fact that you made an effort to ensure that you did not infringe on others will act in your favor in the event your design actually does. This would be considered by the court when deciding what, if any, damages to award.

Implementation

5

IN A NUTSHELL

- Consistency is the most important guideline to follow when implementing the corporate identity program.

- While the logo should be displayed prominently, it should be displayed wisely.

- If you help your client accomplish its new identity implementation prudently, you may be more likely to maintain the integrity of your design throughout the corporation.

- A design manual can be of great assistance in the roll-out of an identity. For small companies, a "keeper of the image" might suffice if provided a written statement of how the program should be implemented.

- Don't give up expressing credibility traits in lieu of finding a common ground with specific audiences in given situations. The company should strive to maintain its established credibility in all it does.

After all your intense planning and weeks of development, everyone is finally happy with the new logo design. But you're not finished yet. The next step is its implementation. You should help your client to not blow it now by just haphazardly sticking the new symbol on anything and everything. Consistency is the most important guideline in implementation.

Remind your client that it should consider every area of public contact an opportunity for logo exploitation (Figures 5–1 through 5–4). With credibility persuasion, each opportunity is a marketing communications opportunity. But while your client should display its logo prominently, it should also display it wisely (Figures 5–5 and 5–7). For instance, a fine-jewelry store would not want to use a

5–1

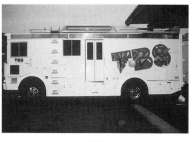

5–2

FIGURES 5–1, 5–2, 5–3, 5–4. Tokyo Broadcast System, Japan's leading broadcast network, demonstrates an astute awareness of the marketing value of its logo by wisely and attractively applying it on everything from a micro radio to vehicles.

5–3

5–4

5–5

5–6

5–7

FIGURES 5–5, 5–6, 5–7. *The dignity of this identity for the Department of Health & Human Services is maintained in every application, from its Spanish-language version, through to a presidential backdrop.*

rough-looking recycled paper prominently featuring your elegant logo for its stationery. You'd think that was just common sense. But remember—*you're* the expert on the client's corporate image team. It's up to you to guide it in the new logo's proper usage.

Table 5–1 lists some common areas (depending on the type of business) for logo display. Of course, there are many more, but those listed in the table should stimulate some ideas for your client, plus serve as a checklist for your client's usage needs both now and in the future.

Opportunities for Logo Display

The following is a compilation of only some of the more common uses for the logo in a corporate identity program.

Printed Pieces

1. Letterhead. Possibly "monarch-size" or smaller, executive-style letterhead, also. Though the second sheets are often blank, you may want to be different and use a light shading or watermark of the logo here.

2. Business cards.

3. Business forms. Press-release forms, fax cover sheets, memorandums, purchase orders, change orders, invoices, shipping forms, etc. Larger corporations literally have hundreds. (Remember your implementation wall from the planning phase?)

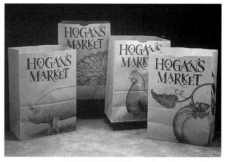

TABLE FIGURE 5–1B

4. Mailing labels and envelopes.

5. Capabilities brochures, pamphlets, catalogs, and booklets.

6. Annual reports.

7. Newsletters.

8. Training literature.

9. Menus.

10. Matchbooks.

11. Shopping bags.

12. Hang tags.

13. Posters.

14. Advertisements.

Rolling Stock

1. Company cars and/or vans.

TABLE FIGURE 5–1A

Table 5–1
(continued)

TABLE FIGURE 5–1C

TABLE FIGURE 5–1D

2. Delivery trucks.

3. Tankers.

4. Railroad cars.

5. Airplanes.

6. Forklifts.

7. Heavy equipment.

Clothing

1. Uniforms (including sports coats, polo shirts, T-shirts, work shirts, etc.)

2. Coveralls.

3. Hats (including hard hats).

4. Aprons.

5. Smocks and lab coats.

6. Name tags.

7. Scarves and ties.

Signage

1. Main exterior.

2. Secondary interior.

3. Directional.

4. Informational.

5. Flags, banners, and pennants.

6. Lobby.

TABLE 5–1
(CONTINUED)

TABLE FIGURE 5–1E

TABLE FIGURE 5–1F

7. Elevator.
8. Doors.

Product Packaging
1. Products.
2. Gift boxes.

3. Wrapping paper and gift tags.
4. Shipping cartons.

Miscellaneous
1. Vending machines.
2. Point-of-purchase displays.
3. Corporate-sponsored tents at various events, such as golf tournaments.
4. Luxury suites (sky boxes) in sports stadiums.
5. Pencils, pens, etc.
6. Promotional giveaways.
7. Trade show exhibits.

Strategies That Will Keep Your Logo Powerful

There are several proven techniques and considerations to ensure that your client's symbol retains its power. The first is a basic but often-overlooked one. That is, *always remember to communicate clearly.* Though this seems easy enough, many things can get in the way. Just a few of them are:

- *Visibility.* This one's simple. Is your client's logo placed where it will always be seen (Figure 5–8), or is there a chance that at times it might be blocked from view (Figure 5–9)?

FIGURE 5–8. *Office Depot's identity is always certain to be easily seen.*

FIGURE 5–9. *A company must consider the visibility of its icon in all applications, under all circumstances—even the beauty of nature can work against you sometimes. (Another sign erected near the street fixed this problem.)*

• *The Holistic Approach.* In this day and age when everyone is touting the holistic approach to medicine, it should be easy to remember that this same strategy also holds true when implementing a logo. Treat the whole picture. For instance, take your client's company truck (Figure 5–10). The identity will have much more impact if the whole vehicle becomes a logo message whose layout is as carefully conceived as the client's letterhead system (Figures 5–11 and 5–12).

FIGURE 5–10. *An effective layout must be followed, no matter what sort of application is being used. This is a bad but very common application of graphics on a truck. It doesn't use company identity effectively, nor do any of the elements communicate.*

FIGURE 5–11, 5–12. *Southern California Gas Company applies its logo wisely and effectively in all circumstances, from letterhead to vehicles. The vehicles are moving billboards, effectively promoting the company daily wherever it travels.*

5–11

5–12

- *Space.* Don't bury a logo in the midst of a lot of "visual swill," as one designer likes to call it (Figure 5–13). Instead, surround your logo with a lot of white space (Figures 5–14 and 5–15). This way it is sure to stand out.

FIGURE 5–13. *If you have any doubt about what "visual swill" means, this sign should make it clear—that's about the only thing it communicates.*

FIGURE 5–14. *Even this small business recognizes how white space can affect legibility. But do they only repair brown shoes?*

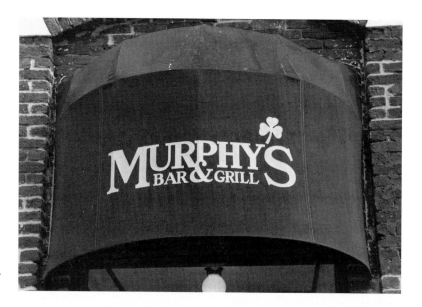

FIGURE 5–15. *Simple, attractive, effective.*

FIGURE 5–16. *In this example, a nice logotype is partially obscured by raising the lettering off its background, creating shadows.*

- *Materials.* Some materials, especially for signage, work better than others. Remind your client to avoid materials that fade or crack under diverse weather conditions. Good quality is an important investment for the long run. Also, the client should avoid using raised letters if possible. This ends up creating a shadow effect, blurring the letters (Figure 5–16) and reducing their communicative effectiveness.

- *Reproduction Art.* Advise your client to always use the logo
saved on disks or camera-ready art, such as Veloxes, for reproduction purposes. Warn the client about the poor reproduction
quality that will result if a logo is hastily cut from their letterhead or business card and used as art for a huge printing project.

The $$$ Side of Implementation

Implementing its new identity can cost your client millions of dollars. As such, you may find it wanting to cut corners and not follow
through on your carefully conceived and approved roll-out strategy.
However, you can offer several suggestions to help your client accomplish implementation prudently, while maintaining the integrity of its new identity.

The general rule is to use up all existing printed material,
which should help cost-wise. (It's also environmentally responsible.)
Also, advise the client to implement in priorities, based on cost,
starting with those that have greatest exposure or ability to achieve
company goals. You might show how to realize savings by: printing
in bulk; reminding them to always consider whether a black-and-
white version of the logo will work just as effectively as full-color; explaining whether screen printing, embroidering, or some other
method might be the better way to apply their logo to employee uniforms; using cost-effective signage materials; and so on. It may take
more research on your part, but it could result in not only cost savings that your client will greatly appreciate, but a long-term relationship in which you serve as the client's implementation management
consultant.

The Design Standards Manual

It's possible that your client may need you to stay on as a consultant through the implementation process and/or create a design manual to outline the logo's application in all possible situations. This is especially useful if the company has many offices or affiliates spread across the nation or world.

The manual's purpose is to preserve the intent of the graphic design program over the long term (Figure 5–17) and, as stated earlier, the long distance (Figure 5–18, pages 87–89). People leave, management relocates, and designers move. The design manual summarizes your identity's planning, the strategy of the logo design, approved Pantone Matching System® colors, dimensions, and typical approved applications. The manual is often loose-leaf, so it can be added to as needed.

Very small businesses may not need a design manual. Instead, it may be better for them to appoint a key person as "keeper of the image." You may want to push for this with fervor, plus provide them with a concise-but-thorough written statement of how that design program should be maintained. It's a shame to see great logo programs fall apart because of lackadaisical control.

Persuasion and Common Ground

Wisdom says that people of the same age, ethnic background, gender, and so on will be more persuasive with one another. However, your client should never give up expressing its credibility traits even if it means losing this common ground. Credibility persuasion requires that the company always projects its own expertise and trustworthiness. If these happen to be traits common to the audience, so much the better.

But with credibility persuasion, it is not necessary for your client to achieve common ground with its audience to influence that audience. Define your client, then retain its credible look at all times.

**THE FIRST HAWAIIAN BANK
SIGNATURE**

Signature Format A

Signature Format B

Signature Format C

First Hawaiian Bank

Signature Format D

The First Hawaiian Signature

All First Hawaiian signatures are comprised of a custom rendered logotype and symbol, arranged either in a "stacked" configuration or in a single line.

The preferred signature presentation is a controlled, or "boxed" format field. These approved signatures are referred to as Format A and Format B, respectively.

The shape of the Format A symbol field cannot be altered. The Format B signature field can be lengthened left or right.

Signature Formats C and D are unboxed versions of the preferred signature formats. At this time, these restricted-use signatures will be used mostly for branch signs and for situations that cannot take a solid background color.

FIGURE 5–17A, 5–17B, AND 5–17C. *This bank uses its design standards manual to explain all aspects of its graphics program to employees and vendors.*

2

5–17A

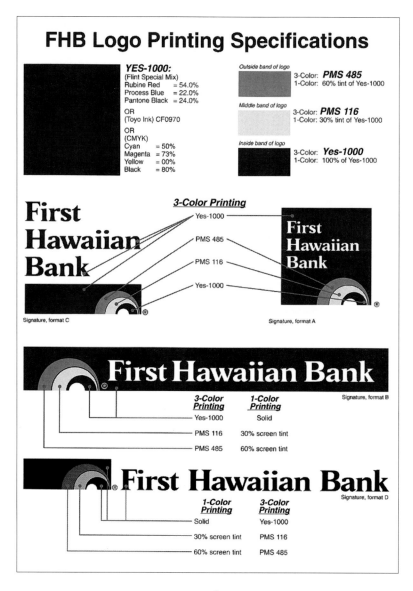

FHB Logo Printing Specifications

YES-1000:
(Flint Special Mix)
Rubine Red = 54.0%
Process Blue = 22.0%
Pantone Black = 24.0%

OR
(Toyo Ink) CF0970

OR
(CMYK)
Cyan = 50%
Magenta = 73%
Yellow = 00%
Black = 80%

Outside band of logo
3-Color: **PMS 485**
1-Color: 60% tint of Yes-1000

Middle band of logo
3-Color: **PMS 116**
1-Color: 30% tint of Yes-1000

Inside band of logo
3-Color: **Yes-1000**
1-Color: 100% of Yes-1000

3-Color Printing

Yes-1000
PMS 485
PMS 116
Yes-1000

Signature, format C

Signature, format A

Signature, format B

3-Color Printing	1-Color Printing
Yes-1000	Solid
PMS 116	30% screen tint
PMS 485	60% screen tint

Signature, format D

1-Color Printing	3-Color Printing
Solid	Yes-1000
30% screen tint	PMS 116
60% screen tint	PMS 485

5–17B

Univers Condensed light
ABCDEFGHIJKLMNOPQRSTUVWXYZ
abcdefghijklmnopqrstuvwxyz 1234567890

Univers Condensed light italic
ABCDEFGHIJKLMNOPQRSTUVWXYZ
abcdefghijklmnopqrstuvwxyz 1234567890

Univers Condensed
ABCDEFGHIJKLMNOPQRSTUVWXYZ
abcdefghijklmnopqrstuvwxyz 1234567890

Univers Condensed italic
ABCDEFGHIJKLMNOPQRSTUVWXYZ
abcdefghijklmnopqrstuvwxyz 1234567890

Univers Condensed bold
ABCDEFGHIJKLMNOPQRSTUVWXYZ
abcdefghijklmnopqrstuvwxyz 1234567890

Univers Condensed bold italic
ABCDEFGHIJKLMNOPQRSTUVWXYZ
abcdefghijklmnopqrstuvwxyz 1234567890

Support Typography

Typestyle consistency, particularly in signature application materials, is essential to projecting a consistent and recognizable First Hawaiian design style. The Univers Condensed type family has been selected as the primary support typestyle and will be specified for use on particular stationery, forms, signs and other communication system materials. As shown in the signature / address block construction below, the neutral "sans serif" style does not compete with the logotype style, and is readily available is a wide range of weights and styles.

To satisfy a wide range of advertising and other print communication requirements, contrasting serif typestyles may be used in combination with the Univers, but must be approved by the Marketing Division.

First Hawaiian Bank
P.O. Box 3200
Honolulu, Hawaii 96847
Telephone (808) 525-6100
Fax (808) 525-1234

First Hawaiian Bank
P.O. Box 3200
Honolulu, Hawaii 96847
Telephone (808) 525-6100
Fax (808) 525-1234

First Hawaiian Bank

First Hawaiian Bank
P.O. Box 3200 Honolulu, Hawaii 96847
Telephone (808) 525-6100 Fax (808) 525-1234

13

FIGURE 5–18A, 5–18B, AND 5–18C. *A design standards manual is vital to maintaining the integrity of an identity program when a company has international branches or affiliates. Coca-Cola uses manuals to explain its logo program in a wide variety of circumstances, and a wide variety of cultures. This manual demonstrates the correct method for using the logo in Olympic Games sponsorships. As the International Olympics Committee is among the most diligent defenders of its logo's integrity, and places many restrictions on how the Five Rings may be used, Coca-Cola's guidelines most certainly proved especially helpful.*

5–18A

BRAND COCA-COLA® CLASSIC/USA

Paralympic StarFire/Brand Coca-Cola® classic composite logo

The Paralympic StarFire/Brand Coca-Cola classic composite logo is to be used only in association with the brand or product. It should never be used to represent The Coca-Cola Company. (A separate composite logo is available for The Coca-Cola Company and the Paralympic logo, see page 16.)

For reproduction in one, two, four or full color application, use the appropriate logomark.

The following trademark notice or "legal line" should be used at the bottom of coupons, point of purchase material and other advertising materials.

© 1995 The Coca-Cola Company. "Coca-Cola," the Red Disk Icon and the Contour Bottle design are trademarks of The Coca-Cola Company.

A registration notice ® is part of the logo and should not be deleted.

COLOR SEPARATIONS

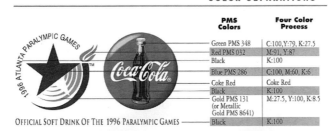

	PMS Colors	Four Color Process
	Green PMS 348	C:100, Y:79, K:27.5
	Red PMS 032	M:91, Y:87
	Black	K:100
	Blue PMS 286	C:100, M:60, K:6
	Coke Red	Coke Red
	Black	K:100
	Gold PMS 131 (or Metallic Gold PMS 8641)	M:27.5, Y:100, K:8.5
	Black	K:100

OFFICIAL SOFT DRINK OF THE 1996 PARALYMPIC GAMES

4 Color

Gold PMS 131
Blue PMS 286
Coke Red
Black

OFFICIAL SOFT DRINK OF THE 1996 PARALYMPIC GAMES

2 Color

Black
Coke Red
Black

OFFICIAL SOFT DRINK OF THE 1996 PARALYMPIC GAMES

1 Color

OFFICIAL SOFT DRINK OF THE 1996 PARALYMPIC GAMES

12

LOGOMARK ON A TONAL BACKGROUND

When the logomark is placed on a background that does not match the color of the Paralympic StarFire logo, then the logomark can be reproduced in full color as depicted here. It is required that a thin white outline be added around the Red Disk Icon.

LOGOMARK ON A COKE RED BACKGROUND

When the logomark is placed on a Coke Red background, the logomark may be reproduced as shown here with the Paralympic StarFire logo in either All White or All Black. It is required that a thin white outline be added around the Red Disk Icon.

PARALYMPIC PICTOGRAMS

The full set of Paralympic pictograms are available upon request. Contact Jody Trimmer in the Olympic Marketing Department.

Basketball   **Swimming**   **Tennis**

13

Don't change it for each customer who walks through the door. Likewise, the well-designed logo does not need to change for different publics nationally or internationally. Remember: An airline doesn't change the logo on its tail for every city or country to which it travels.

In the end, the best logos are not just memorable images that readily bring their company or product to mind—that's the brick-and-mortar function of any logo. Logos that are truly persuasive—those developed according to the principles of credibility persuasion—will express the company's attributes both in their design and in their usage. You may need to occasionally "tweak" things here and there as the client's business objectives and styles change, but even minor alterations should be based on established objectives and design criteria so the identity does not become corrupted over time. Your credibility-based logo system should continue to work for your client for many years.

Case Studies

FIGURE 6–1.

Presbyterian Church (USA)

Challenge: Create an official seal and symbol for a reunited church
order that would satisfy the needs of the three previous sects that
were joining again after 122 years of separation (Figure 6–1).

Client: Presbyterian Church (USA)

Design firm: Malcolm Grear Designers, Providence, RI

In the late nineteenth century, the Presbyterian Church split into
three parts, each with its own symbol. In 1958, two of those sections
joined to form the United Presbyterian Church in the United
States. Finally in 1983, after 122 years of separation, the remaining
division reunited with the others to form the Presbyterian Church
(USA). Among their first actions was to seek a new symbol and seal.
A committee of nine people was formed to oversee this, comprised
of representatives from all three former factions. Not surprisingly,
there were differences to be ironed out.

  Still, they agreed on several things. Among the most important
were that the new symbol's design had to include fire, the cross, a
descending dove, and a book; it had to be applicable in both two
and three dimensions, in all media; it should be formal; it must have

continuity with "the historic symbols of the Reformed tradition and the larger Christian tradition," but also be contemporary; and it had to be a symbol whose qualities would not be exhausted at first glance. Along with gaining the design committee's approval, the symbol would have to earn the acceptance of, first, the 2500 members of the church's general assembly; second, a 40-member board; and then a 700-member governing board, which had the final say.

He knew it was an awesome challenge, but principal Malcolm Grear of Malcolm Grear Designers (MGD), which won the project after a search involving more than 600 original candidates, was undaunted. In fact, that was the reason his firm so wanted the assignment. A logo design is one of the most sophisticated projects a designer can undertake, Grear believes, and since symbolism is so vital to a church's soul, in this project that sophistication would be greatly intensified.

The client had much research to hand over by the time it called in MGD. Part of this advance thinking had to do with the fact that the church had already nearly approved—then at the last minute rejected—a symbol from another designer. The rejection was not due to what the designer presented: It was a result of the church learning, from the response of members nationwide, that the new

FIGURE 6–2. *When he told the church that his firm would create thousands of preliminary sketches for its project, Malcolm Grear got a surprise— the head of the church's design committee wanted to actually count them. He stopped at 5000.*

symbol was very important to all. In order for it to gain wide acceptance, it needed to be developed with the utmost consideration.
That's when the church got serious and formed its design committee.

While the church had many dictates regarding the design of its
symbol, in fact it was working out its own theological affirmation
during the process—much like the business organizations in the
painful process of restructuring that Debra Kelley discussed earlier
in this book (see page 33). MGD employed the same questionnaire
(shown in Chapter 3 on page 56) that it uses for other clients to get
the committee (which Grear called the "most intellectually sophisticated" he'd ever worked with) in a discussion of their exact wants
and needs. MGD then began its design process not by designing,
but by hiring a theological art historian as a consultant, to help
them explore the depths and range of Christian symbols that could
be used in the new seal.

Then they sat down to design. Thousands of ideas later, the firm
developed a logo that, in spite of the numbers who had to agree on
it in the approval process, quickly and easily gained the respect of all
(Figures 6–2 through 6–8). It was so treasured that the church has
written a book, *Sealed in Christ,* by John M. Mulder, devoted
entirely to the symbol's development and its significance.

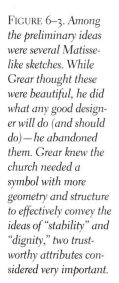

FIGURE 6–3. *Among
the preliminary ideas
were several Matisse-
like sketches. While
Grear thought these
were beautiful, he did
what any good design-
er will do (and should
do)—he abandoned
them. Grear knew the
church needed a
symbol with more
geometry and structure
to effectively convey the
ideas of "stability" and
"dignity," two trust-
worthy attributes con-
sidered very important.*

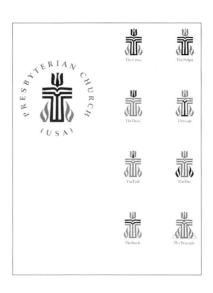

FIGURE 6–4. *The client told Grear it needed a symbol that represented four things: the cross, fire, a dove, and the Book. The solution gave the church all that and more.*

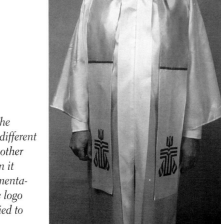

FIGURE 6–5. *The church was no different than clients in other businesses when it came to implementation needs. The logo had to be applied to "uniforms."*

FIGURE 6–6. *It had to work on "banners."*

FIGURE 6–7. *It needed to be effective on exterior signage.*

FIGURE 6–8. *It needed to work well when executed in various materials.*

FIGURE 6–9.

Designing in the Same Category: How to Keep it Fresh

Challenge: Create unique identities for clients in the same or a closely related field. (Figure 6–9)

Client: Various

Type of business: High technological

Design firm: Hornall Anderson Design Works, Seattle, WA

Hornall Anderson Design Works (HADW), famous worldwide for its Starbucks Coffee designs, also attracts many clients in the technology industry, from telecommunications conglomerates to software manufacturers, and everyone in between. As is often the case, a client in a certain business arena will come to HADW because of work it has seen it do for another company in the same field. The trick, then, is for HADW to create a distinctive identity for each of these companies when their credibility traits are likely to overlap.

Partner Jack Anderson says that his firm starts by ensuring the company's (or product's) name sounds different. If one is called Intermation (Figure 6–10) and another Midcom (Figure 6–11), and they're both in technology, having the names sound different helps a lot. Using different letterforms if you're doing a wordmark also can go a long way in distinguishing the client (Figures 6–12 and 6–13).

6–10

MIDC**O**M

6–11

FIGURES 6–10, 6–11. *Developing distinctive names is the first step in developing identities that differentiate clients who operate in the same marketing category. In this case, both are in communications technology: Intermation (6–10) is a data storage and retrieval company, while Midcom Communications (6–11) resells telephone services.*

6–12

6–13

FIGURES 6–12, 6–13. *Using very different letterforms for those names is the next step. McCaw provides wireless services internationally; Nextlink is a telecommunications provider. Note how the treatment of the x reflects Nextlink's continuing leap into the future of technology.*

Another way to attain a distinctive mark is to avoid trendy techniques that are apparent in the client's industry. Once you take the doors off the perception of what a technical logo should look like, you can create something that is unique, Anderson said. Still, that isn't always easy. It's impossible not to be influenced by these devices, especially when the public so readily identifies them with their particular industry.

Fortunately, many high-tech companies are turning away from the hard, sterile, technical, precision-engineering driven mark that everyone was doing before. "There are a lot of those out there, and there are a lot of companies that don't have a face and a personality because of it," Anderson said. Instead, companies are now focusing on the benefits technology gives them, as opposed to the technology itself.

That was the emphasis behind the Corbis logo (Figure 6–14)— a warmer, more organic, engaging feeling, achieved by applying some of the same aesthetic sensibilities that might have been used

C O R B I S

FIGURE 6–14. *The word* corbis *is Latin for* woven basket *or* container. *So the distinct identity for this digital-image archive is given a jump start by the organic nature of its name. HADW's design portrays the company's main business, the swirling motion connotes Corbis's CD products, and the grainy texture works well on the many applications it must accommodate.*

for a gardening logo, artist's studio, or a grocery market. The word *corbus* means "woven basket" or "container" in Latin, so the name itself conjured up the solution.

Apple did this a long time ago, Anderson reminds us, not so much by how it delineated the apple, but by using the icon of an apple in a technological industry. At the time, most computer-based businesses were following IBM's lead, using hard-edged type and horizontal lines, such as the first Microsoft logo: a sterile, all-uppercase, sans serif font striped in a Venetian-blind mode.

HADW believes that whenever a designer can resist the expected technique or vocabulary for the category, the more unique the logo will be. However, don't take it too far out or your logo, though truly unique, may be inappropriate. You must walk the line between what is *different* and what is *appropriate*. A logo can't be totally disconnected to the category your client is in; it has to somehow educate viewers as to that category (Figure 6–15). A balancing act must go on.

FIGURE 6–15. *While you want to make your mark distinctive by not relying too much on the tried-and-true, you also don't want to stray so far from the norm that the mark fails to educate viewers regarding the nature of the business.*

Figure 6–16.

A Unified Character Through "Multiple Personalities"

Challenge: Create an identity for a major cable movie network that uses multiple images to suit the various types of movies being shown, while maintaining a unified character (Figure 6–16).

Client: Turner Classic Movies

Type of business: Cable movie network

Design firm: Charles S. Anderson Design Company, Minneapolis, MN

Not all projects can be guided by the findings of your research, no matter how hard you try. Yet you learn to make the best of them, as Charles S. Anderson Design Company (CSA) has learned. A classic example is offered by Turner Classic Movies. Turner Broadcasting Corporation needed an identity for a new movie channel that would be shown on cable television. The channel would feature nothing but classics, hence the name Turner Classic Movies (TCM). So they called two design firms that specialize in animated graphics—and they called CSA.

There were several challenges with this project, beginning with the client wanting CSA to submit ideas before it decided on a firm; principal Charles Anderson figured that spelled spec work. As it turned out, however, TCM was willing to pay for them. Anderson was also told the two other firms were presenting scores of design solutions. While CSA's shortlist is normally a true shortlist—he typically offers three or four solutions—in the end the firm agreed to show about 30 possibilities, due to the volume of work the winner would gain (everything from the actual mark to mailers, promotional materials, posters, etc.)

The client's selection method is a good example of what can happen when it is not truly cognizant of the importance of its signature. Which firm won the project all came down to a lunchroom survey. Their various ideas were pinned to the bulletin board in the employees' lunchroom; the one that received the most "votes" won. CSA's design emerged with the most checkmarks—although, Anderson said, they picked "the worst of the lot"—a character in a top hat.

Still, that gave CSA a shot at applying some true design methodology to develop something that the client, the design firm, and the lunchroom balloters would be happy with. TCM was looking for only one mark. Given that there were many different categories of films in the vast stock of archives Turner had assembled—everything from detective flicks to musicals to monster movies—CSA convinced Turner to let them create more character logos. As the designs progressed, and more and more characters emerged, they came to symbolize the categories of movies the station would air (Figure 6–17). In the end, they ended up with 50 different characters, from movie stars indicative of movie types, to viewers' reactions (such as a yawning man), to characters representing movie blitzes (such as a "mom," for a Mother's Day movie weekend special).

Next, CSA determined the client would need different formats to accommodate the scales of the icons on screen. Sometimes, one

FIGURE 6–17. Some businesses require more than one logo to serve their needs, especially one like a television network. CSA created over 50 heads to serve as symbols for Turner Classic Movies; each represents a different movie category, weekend movie blitz, or viewer's response. Yet there is continuity throughout, maintained by the style in which the characters are drawn.

would be shown in the right bottom corner of the television screen to identify the station, so it needed to be small. Other times the same head would need to be large, such as when introducing the start-up of a movie in its category. Four different formats were eventually developed (Figure 6–18). By the end of the project, that one logo assignment had evolved into 200 variations (with TCM itself taking on the design of even more).

In spite of the number of icons being used, there is a consistency in the look. This is provided by the way each icon is drawn: a heavy, black-and-white stylized head, simply executed so it will translate well on screen and in a host of other applications (Figures 6–19, 6–20, and 6–21). Though the characters themselves are simple, Anderson says their creation was anything but. "They were hard to do because we were trying to create an identifiable character [such

as Fred Astaire, representing the musical category], yet keep them
simple at the same time," he explained.

What works for the client and what earns the respect of peers is
not always the same. Anderson admits that he doesn't know if his
solution "is a favorite of designers." Nevertheless, viewers like the
characters, the icons do the job well, and they keep the station from
becoming boring—an especially important point for a medium that
is all about motion and change, where a static identity has little or
no impact.

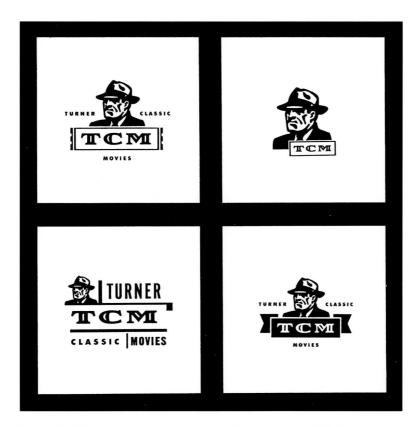

FIGURE 6–18. *Four formats accommodate the different scales in which the logos must appear on the television screen.*

6–19

6–20

6–21

Figure 6–19. *TCM letterhead.*

Figure 6–20. *TCM business cards cleverly play off movie tickets and via the format of the cards themselves reflect the company's business.*

Figure 6–21. *The symbols are perfect for adorning a variety of products (shown are commemorative pins and tins) and are popular with consumers. When TCM asked CSA to sign over the rights for such usage, CSA complied— after it negotiated a buy-out of rights for the symbols' use on products TCM sells for profit.*

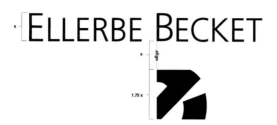

FIGURE 6–22.

Ellerbe Becket

Challenge: Develop a new identity for a well-established international firm undergoing restructuring (Figure 6–22).

Client: Ellerbe Becket

Type of business: Architecture, engineering, and construction

Design firm: Hall Kelley Inc., Marine on St. Croix, MN

This well-established and respected architectural firm, with offices worldwide, was undergoing a restructuring in which it was focusing on a broader mix of turnkey services. Though the company had been in business since 1909 and had what Hall Kelley principal Debra Kelley calls a "wonderfully designed proposal system," Ellerbe Becket had no true logo. Instead, it had an *almost* standard typographical method for its name that bordered on a logotype, an outgrowth of its elegant proposal system, but there was no consistency in how it was used. It was also weak when not the primary piece of information on a page, and it was difficult to apply in all the ways this international company needed. Plus, it did not reflect the company's construction and engineering services. Ellerbe Becket recognized that the restructuring was a perfect time to firm up its identity.

When Hall Kelley Inc. was called into the project, it began as it always does: with an intense stage of research and planning, using every tool from surveying management, employees, and the client's external public, to combing through all the client's market research, taking inventory on what computer systems and graphic and technical resources were available within the company, and conducting its own specially developed "Chair Test" (described in Chapter 3 on pages 53–55). They do this not only to gather a cross section of information, but because it involves a wide spectrum of thought and participation from the client which makes it more likely the solution will be acceptable by everyone within the company. This stage often proves fruitful not just for the design firm, but for the client, also. In the process of defining itself so the designers can translate that visually, the client often solidifies its own new direction.

In time, three credibility traits emerged. Ellerbe Becket recognized that it was, and wanted to be:

1. A valued advisor to its clients.

2. An innovator.

3. A firm of breadth, depth, and history, able to undertake massive and complex challenges on an international scale.

That understanding enabled Hall Kelley to develop a mark that could project these traits, maintain a consistent image from one application to the next, and incorporate Ellerbe Becket's focus not just on architecture, but engineering and construction as well. The new logotype (Figure 6–23) was set in a slightly modified version of Humanist 777, whose elegant forms give it an unadorned timelessness. The mark was based on the letter *e* (chosen because of its versatility and relationship to the name Ellerbe Becket), rolled on its side in a 45-degree angle for interest, and partially obscured from view as if it were behind a window (Figure 6–24). The new logo reflects all the company's services, and is easily applied to a variety of situations.

To help Ellerbe Becket implement its new program, Hall Kelley created a design manual (Figures 6–25 and 6–26). Then it

ELLERBE BECKET

FIGURE 6–23. *Ellerbe Becket's new, elegant logotype (Humanist 777, also called Frutiger light) has an unadorned timelessness.*

went one step further. Because the client has offices across the world, Hall Kelley developed an interactive identity show that was taken on the road to introduce and familiarize everyone with the new identity (Figures C–1 through C–7). This latter step is often crucial to the success of an identity, Kelley remarked. "Identity is a process that needs to be worked through. People must understand who and what they are, then we as designers visually articulate that. But we can't stop there. They are adopting a visual symbol of who they are. We need to help them accept it."

FIGURE 6–24. *The mark reflects the architectural nature of Ellerbe Becket. Partially obstructing the e makes it appear as if it is being viewed from behind a window.*

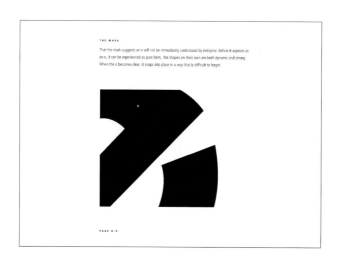

THE MARK

That the mark suggests an e will not be immediately understood by everyone. Before it appears as an e, it can be experienced as pure form, the shapes on their own are both dynamic and strong. When the e becomes clear, it snaps into place in a way that is difficult to forget.

PAGE A-5

The identity incorporates a mark that is based on the letter e. More literal marks were seen as too restrictive to a firm as broad as Ellerbe Becket. The e was chosen because of its versatility and relationship to the name Ellerbe Becket.

A capital e in the typeface Goudy (shown here) is authoritative and has a traditional elegance about it.

Lowercase letters generally feel more youthful and energetic.

In the typeface Franklin Gothic #2, the e is a more simple shape, it is more pure and elemental. It also has visual weight, something that will be helpful later.

Lower case e's are interesting in that they suggest a face. This human aspect is intriguing for a service firm. The face is revealed if something's added, like a pair of glasses.

Another interesting aspect of this lowercase e is that it can roll, suggesting movement, change, or process.

6–25

FIGURES 6–25, 6–26. *The design manual, distributed to Ellerbe Becket's offices world-wide, explains not just how the new look should be used, but how and why it was created. This was done so that all would recognize and under-stand the need for the new identity.*

The challenge was to find a way to make the e into a unique and memorable shape that would be bold, energetic, sophisticated and unique.

And yet this lower case e, on its own, cannot represent Ellerbe Becket for two reasons: It is too generic and therefore cannot belong to the firm. And it suggests a personality that is not always appropriate.

A rectangle is a logical additional element. It visually contrasts the roundness of the e.

When a part of the e is seen "behind" the rectangle, the latter shape suggests an architectural element: a window. The e quietly suggests the human element.

By adding the rolling aspect to the e, a strong diagonal is introduced and the two interesting shapes emerge.

The rectangle can now be dropped. There is more pleasure in this economy of an implied rectangle.

6–26

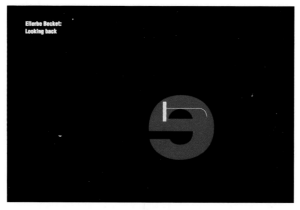

C–1

C–2

FIGURES C–1, C–2, C–3, C–4, C–5, C–6, C-7. *The interactive computer show Hall Kelley Inc. created for Ellerbe Becket traveled to all the firm's offices worldwide. It explained why the new identity was created as well as how it was done. Promoting this understanding corporate-wide not only helped everyone buy into the new identity, but also meant that it was more likely the program's integrity would be maintained.*

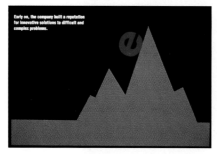

C–3

C–4

C–5

C–6

C–7

From Now to Eternity: A Showcase of Power

As you review the following examples of credibility-based logo design, notice the numerous ways in which the company business is treated graphically to achieve an outstanding combination of credibility, personality, and aesthetics. (Figures C–8 through C–40 and 5–27 through 5–116.) Remember: look "expert" by symbolizing the company business. Look "trustworty" with an interesting design form, reflecting confidence in the company's integrity and reliability of important attributes.

FIGURE C–8. Color adds a strong message to a logo if, once again, it is applied wisely. These logos represent various possibilities for using color. C–8, created for the City of Phoenix, shows how even a single color can have great impact. It is also a cost-efficient choice, something that is often important to a government group, which relies on taxpayers for funding. (Smit Ghormley Lofgreen Design)

SAN FRANCISCO
INTERNATIONAL
FILM FESTIVAL

FIGURE C–9. This logo uses two colors with a registration that is not critical. (Primo Angeli Inc.)

FIGURE C–10. *The Lucca logo seems simple enough, but the registration is critical and the logo also gets an embossed treatment when used on letterhead.* (Primo Angeli Inc.)

FIGURE C–11. *The symbol for Cochran-Char interior designers uses a two-color design whose registration is critical. Silver foil completes the look.* (Bud Linschoten)

…2. A good-looking uniform,
…efully embellished with the
…pany logo, can be often
…rlooked yet significant
…tributor in boosting
…ployee morale. This
…ractive outfit is worn by
…kers at the Southern
…lifornia Gas Company
…ssman/Prejza Design &
…, Inc.)

FIGURE C–13. *Using*
color to turn the letters
in this rock group's
logo back on them-
selves offers an
interesting identity
solution. (Pinkhaus)

C–14

FIGURES C–14, C–15. *Each product in Starbucks Coffee's lineup has its own name and look, yet the feel of the original product (C–14) is maintained through-out (C–15) to link their identities.* (Hornall Anderson Design Works)

C–15

C–16

FIGURES C–16, C–17. *The choice of colors for these two attractive logos sends very different messages to viewers about the nature of the television networks. Graphics in Japan are often playful, even when aimed at adult audiences. The TBS logo aptly reflects this.* (C–16, Chermayeff & Geismar; C–17, Shimokochi/Reeves)

C–17

FIGURE C–18. *The symbol for Sara Lee Corporation's Olympic Partnership immediately links the organization to the Olympics via its color choice and the single ring.* (Pinkhaus)

C–19

FIGURES C–19, C–20.
*The single color chosen
for The Masonry
Company logo is a
wise decision, not just
because it plays off the
bricks used in masonry,
but because of the
variety of applications
the logo must
accommodate.* (Smit
Ghormley Lofgreen
Design)

C–20

FIGURE C–21. *Energy
and fun are imparted
through the choice of
color and type used for
this travel agent's
symbol.* (Max Davis
Company N.A.)

PACIFIC HARBOR
travel
inc.

FIGURES C–22, C–23A, C–23B. *The Rock 'n' Roll Hall of Fame's logo had to appeal to age groups from children through senior citizens. Plus, it needed to adorn many products as well as be applicable in a variety of identity implementations (letterhead, signage, etc.). The solution, playing off both the shape of the Hall of Fame building and a guitar, works equally well in color or black and white, for all its many needs.* (Nesnadny + Schwartz)

C–22

C–23A

C–23B

FIGURE C–24. *Pepsi Stuff is a promotional campaign for Pepsi products. The identity with the main product is readily established through both the logo's color and the name.* (Pinkhaus)

FIGURE C–25. *Lipton Tennis Championships is a world-class tennis tournament recently begun in Miami.* (Pinkhaus)

FIGURE C–26. *The well-recognized red ribbon worn to remind people of the AIDS crisis is put to good use in this unpretentious, but profound, symbol created for an AIDS fundraising walk-athon.* (Drive Communications)

FIGURE C–27. *Color can be much more than adornment. Here, it is key to representing the various racial groups that this St. Paul, Minnesota-based organization seeks to unite.* (Hall Kelley Inc.)

FIGURE C–28. *Attitude, color, textures, and design style are just some of the preferences of its client that Hornall Anderson Design Works seeks to uncover through its use of "attitude boards."* (Hornall Anderson Design Works)

FIGURE C–29. *Deleo Clay Tiles' logo appropriately relies on the earthtones associated with its products, as well as an illustration style and icons that imply old-fashioned craftsmanship.* (Mires Design)

FIGURE C–30. *The pastels that have come to represent Florida, and Miami in particular, are employed in this restaurant logo that says as much about the attitude of the restaurant as it does about the menu offerings.* (Pinkhaus)

C–31

FIGURES C–31, C–32. *The National Football League Players Association is the umbrella organization under which Players Inc., the NFLPA's marketing arm, operates. The connection is evident through both the style of the illustrations used in the two logos and their coloration.* (Grafik Communications Inc.)

C–32

FIGURE C–33. *The bright colors of this symbol make a great attention grabber, and probably lead to many product sales for the client.* (Mires Design)

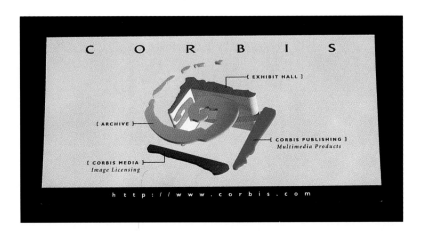

FIGURE C–34. *This is an announcement for Corbis's site on the World Wide Web. The applications for logos continue to broaden as new technology is developed and creates more marketing opportunities. For instance, ten years ago who would have thought there would ever be something called the World Wide Web? When creating a logo and speccing color, today's designers must be almost clairvoyant to predict how that logo will be employed and what will make it stand out in future applications.* (Hornall Anderson Design Works)

FIGURE C–35. *The*
logo of The New
Victory Theater, New
York City's first theater
for youth, dynamically
expresses jubilation
through both spirited
colors and the
triumphant V formed
by the figure's arms.
(Chermayeff &
Geismar Inc.)

FIGURE C–36. *When*
speccing color, as with
any other design
component in a logo,
the designer must
consider whether the
palette is a current
trend or one that will
stand the test of time.
This logo is as
appropriate today as it
was when created in
1972. (Bass/Yager
Associates)

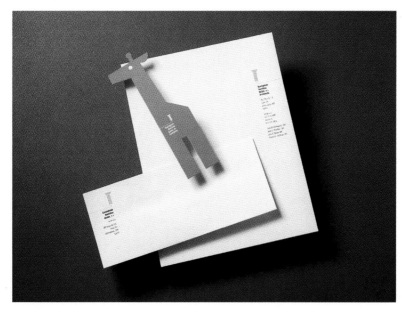

FIGURE C–37. *A*
clever simplicity in
both color choice and
design is the key
behind this logo's
ability to convey its
client's message. (Hall
Kelley Inc.)

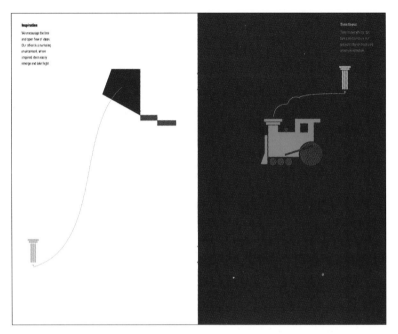

Inspiration

We encourage the free and open flow of ideas. Our office is a nurturing environment, where inspired ideas easily emerge and take flight.

Timeliness

FIGURE C–38. *Unpretentious iconology and vibrant colors soundly and quickly make the points outlined in architectural firm Cuningham Hamilton Quiter's capabilities brochure. The logo cleverly is employed as the narrator of the story.* (Hall Kelley Inc.)

FIGURE C–39. *Color can be used to denote the age group of your market.* (Richards & Swensen)

FIGURE C–40. *The creativity and attitude of this design group is evident in both its logo's color palette and symbolism.* (Shimokochi/Reeves)

FIGURE 6–27. *What sort of message would this down-feather products company's logo send if its Northwestern country backdrop was replaced with a New York City skyline?* (Hornall Anderson Design Works)

FIGURE 6–28. *The Tee Shirt Company is simply and effectively portrayed with this logo.* (Mires Design)

FIGURE 6–29. *Pro Spirit, a line of clothing Target Stores introduced in conjunction with the Summer Games in Atlanta.* (Charles S. Anderson Design Company)

FIGURE 6–30. *Pudding It First is a line of stores that sell—guess what?* (Favermann Design)

FIGURE 6–31. *This logo, created for a channel introducing viewers to all the features of their cable provider, has double meaning via the complementary eye and I. Additionally, the eye can be animated and "reinvented for on-air graphics."* (Firehouse 101 Art + Design)

FIGURE 6–32. *The r logo for Paramount involved a simple cleanup of the existi one.* (Charles S. Anderson Design Company)

FIGURE 6–33. *This logo demonstrates how attractive a well-designed word mark can be. It has the added benefit of applying easily to the many applications necessary for a market.* (Hornall Anderson Design Works)

FIGURE 6–34. *The sides form a W; turned horizontally, you see a B. The entire shape forms a pencil, a memorable icon for Waller Brothers Office Supplies.* (Pentagram NY)

FIGURE 6–35. *The VA logo conveys authority in keeping with its government persona, but in a friendly manner to reflect its function as an agency established to assist veterans.* (Malcolm Grear Designers)

FIGURE 6–36. *Peggy Stern Communication—attractive, clever, effective.* (Dale Vermeer Design)

6–37

6–38

FIGURES 6–37, 6–38. *First Night is an annual event held in cities across the United States, with each city responsible for developing its own logo. Notice how the stylized feel of Honolulu's logo (the moon is applied in silver foil) is consistent with the stylized, Matisse-like tone of the umbrella organization (6–38, right).* (6–37, Bud Linschoten; 6–38, Favermann Design)

FIGURE 6–39. *This logo for Arrow, the world's largest distributor of electronic components and computer products, is drawn to look like a printed circuit. However, the design concept resides in the O. The two squiggly lines (representing the suppliers and manufacturers) link to form the O and the word* arrow. *(Waters Design Associates)*

FIGURE 6–40. *This logo wisely borrows from the asp of the American Medical Association's logo to form a C and an A for Clay Adams, a division of Becton, Dickinson and Company hospital supplies. (Chermayeff & Geismar Inc.)*

FIGURE 6–41. *Errands Unlimited's clever logo is memorable, self-explanatory, and easy to implement.* (Bud Linschoten)

FIGURE 6–42. *This striking abstract mark combines an eye and an* e *to represent Time Warner's main enterprises: media and entertainment.* (Chermayeff & Geismar Inc.)

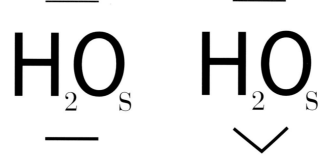

FIGURE 6–43. *Waters Design Associates' logo is a literal translation of the founder's name (John Waters). It also reflects the core activity of the company: translating messages into visual presentations. The addition of the two rules turns the entire mark into a face. This is sometimes presented as a somber expression (left) followed by the smile of surprise (right). The smiling face is used on all basic papers to reflect the company's good nature.* (Waters Design Associates)

Electro Scan

FIGURE 6–44. *Electro Scan's business is readily implied through the scan lines that make up the letters of its logo.* (Malcolm Grear Designers)

FIGURE 6–45. *The French Paper Company logo has made both its company and its creator, Charles S. Anderson, famous, plus almost single-handedly snowballed the Retro movement across the design world. It is appropriate for the company, which is a small, family-owned, friendly mill. (Charles S. Anderson Design Company)*

FIGURE 6–46A AND 6–46B. *This icon, also created for French Paper, departs from Retro and takes on an "industrial" look in support of the line of paper it represents — Dur-O-Tone. However, it still connotes the friendly, quirky nature of French. (Charles S. Anderson Design Company)*

6–46A

6–46B

6–47

6–48

FIGURES 6–47, 6–48, 6–49. *These three examples once again show the various innovative approaches that can be taken to create distinctive, compelling logos for organizations operating in the same category. The protective nature of the Conservation Corps (6–47) is aptly reflected in the way this mother bear nurtures her cub. A very different approach (6–48) is taken for the League of Conservation Voters. Managing the earth's tropical forests is the goal of the not-for-profit Tropical Forest Foundation (6–49). (6–47, VanderByl Design; 6–48 and 6–49, Grafik Communications Inc.)*

6–49

FIGURE 6–50. *Nepco's (which originally stood for New England Printed Tape Company) logo worked even when the company expanded from printing giftwrapping ribbon to fiber-optic materials and moved to the South.* (Malcolm Grear Designers)

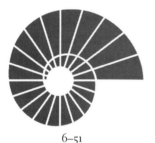

6–51

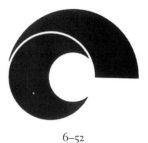

6–52

FIGURES 6–51, 6–52. *Even if you are not current on Turkish affairs, it's easy to see there is a connection between these two logos. The striped version is a logo for Koc University in Istanbul; the solid is for Rahmi M. Koc Industrial Museum, also in Istanbul. The Koc family, whose name means* ram, *are the "Rockefellers" of Turkey.* (Chermayeff & Geismar Inc.)

FIGURE 6–53. *The spicy theme and menu for the dinner party fundraiser sponsored by the American Heart Association in Columbus, Ohio, comes across loud and clear.* (Firehouse 101 Art + Design)

6–54

6–55

FIGURES 6–54, 6–55,
6–56. *Favermann
Design's logos for the
site (6–54) and canoe
events trials (6–55,
6–56) are linked to
each other and to the
logo which was
developed for the
Summer Games in
Atlanta by Landor
Associates.* (Faver-
mann Design)

6–56

FIGURE 6–57. *The elegance of the Mandarin Oriental Hotels is simply and beautifully conveyed in this logo.* (Pentagram NY)

FIGURE 6–58. *The essence of a credibilty-based logo. Roadrunner Records.* (Smit Ghormley Lofgreen)

FIGURES 6–59, 6–60. *These two logos represent two different clothing lines for the same manufacturer. The walking man (6–59) is for Sierra Designs' line of outdoor wear, while the bear (6–60) is for its line of work clothes that can also be worn as casual wear.* (Charles S. Anderson Design Company)

6–59

6–60

FIGURE 6–61. *The L and W of Washington and Lee are masterfully conveyed in the kicker's stance.* (Favermann Design)

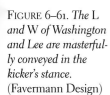

**50 Years of Kicks
1947 ★ 1996**
WASHINGTON & LEE SOCCER

FIGURE 6–62. *Another approach to a soccer-related logo.* (Pentagram NY)

FIGURE 6–63. *The Edge is an alternative rock station in Minneapolis, Minnesota.* (Charles S. Anderson Design Company)

FIGURE 6–64. *Radio Ranch is a commercial production company in Dallas, Texas.* (Pentagram NY)

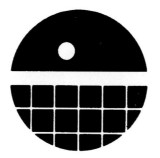

FIGURE 6–65. *Several icons are packed into this simple symbol: the tennis net in the bottom semicircle, the tennis ball floating over the net in the top one, and the entire* O *shape of the logo itself, which can represent either a tennis ball or the* O *in Oahu Racket Club.* (Nick Kaars and Associates)

FIGURE 6–66. *You don't have to suppress your sense of humor to create a great logo, as this creation for Mr. and Mrs. Aubrey Hair demonstrates.* (Pentagram NY)

144 •

FIGURE 6–67.
*Designers are very
familiar with this logo
for PANTONE. The
eye pairs up with a
crown to represent the
visual industry's
premier color
matching system.*
(Charles S. Anderson
Design Company)

FIGURE 6–68. *The
logo for this seafood
company would
express its line of
business even without
the logotype.* (Eric
Woo Design)

FIGURE 6–69. *Truth Decay is a Columbus, Ohio-based alternative rock band that lyrically blends politics and biting sarcasm. Firehouse 101's logo creation aims for a strong point of view from mixed emotional sides by using the positive/negative juxtapositioning along with two hearts (representing the different points of view) and a tongue spitting out a religious icon (sarcasm).* (Firehouse 101 Art + Design)

FIGURE 6–70. *The E formed by the musical notes make up the first letters of Endymion Ensemble.* (Pentagram NY)

FIGURE 6–71. *A similar approach gives us the logo for the House of Music, a music store in Honolulu, Hawaii.* (Bud Linschoten)

FIGURE 6–72. *A contemporary version of a long-standing theatrical icon becomes the logo for Theatre Square.* (VanderByl Design)

THE BECKER GROUP

FIGURE 6–73. *The Becker Group designs holiday decor programs for the retail community. Its logo likewise uses a modern version of a symbol that is synonymous with the holidays.* (Grafik Communications Inc.)

6–74

6–75

6–76

FIGURE 6–74, 6–75, 6–76. *Iconography crosses international boundaries to speak a common language. The logo shown in 6–74 is for Travis Construction; 6–75 is for J. Sadler Company, a home improvement specialist in Virginia. Both companies are in the United States. 6–76 was created for Ferreteria El Potosino, a hardware store operating in Mexico.* (6–74 Pentagram NY; 6–75 Harrisberger Creative; 6–76 Mauro Machuca)

FIGURE 6–77. *Art deco meets the high-tech future in this Pinkhaus logo for Gamut Media, a pairing well suited to this multimedia production studio in Miami.* (Pinkhaus)

FIGURE 6–78. *This logo for Sony E-TV was created for an ad promoting Sony's new technology, digital video.* (Charles S. Anderson Design Company)

FIGURE 6–79. *Century Hawaii Realty required a strong image that would convey personalized services and retain its strength in newspaper ads. The house-and-hand trademark fulfills both needs, plus reflects the contractual agreements of real estate.* (Bud Linschoten)

FIGURE 6–80. *While Bauer Skates' logo doesn't look like Nike's, it is suggestive of the swoosh—appropriate, since Bauer, a hockey and rollerblade products producer, is a Nike division.* (Pinkhaus)

FIGURE 6–81. *A much more traditional approach is used in this logo for Nike Football—with a stylized twist and a little surprise. A second look reveals the Nike swoosh.* (Charles S. Anderson Design Company)

FIGURE 6–82. *This logo cleverly reveals both the company name (Fox River Paper) and the nature of its business through the sheets of paper that make up the fox's head.* (Pentagram NY)

FIGURE 6–83. *An eye is formed by the way the hands connect, conveying how the blind use their hands to see when reading Braille in this compelling logo for the Wichita Industry and Services for the Blind.* (Gardner Design)

FIGURE 6–84. *Picket fences and sawed "boards" make up a logo fit for ARK Fence, a fencing contractor.* (Gardner Design)

FIGURE 6–85.
Bergelectric Corpora-
tion is, as the name
and logo readily
reveal, an electrical
contractor. (The
Weller Institute for the
Cure of Design)

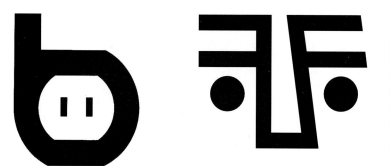

FIGURE 6–85.
Bergelectric Corpora-
tion is, as the name
and logo readily
reveal, an electrical
contractor. (The
Weller Institute for the
Cure of Design)

FIGURE 6–86.
*Faulkner Institute for
Eye Care and Surgery
requested a mark with
a "noncorporate
personal touch." The
one it received also
incorporates "seeing"
and the letter* F. (Bud
Linschoten)

KNOW YOURSELF

FIGURE 6–87. *The strength of this logo comes through its simple articulation of the
Nike-sponsored internal leadership training seminar. The logo was screenprinted on a
mirror, then embedded in a type of rubber that looked like the sole of a tennis shoe.
The mirror was packaged in a box along with information on the seminar, and sent
out to 100 top Nike executives. When they opened it, the first thing they saw was their
own reflection.* (Max Davis Company N.A.)

152 •

FIGURE 6–88. *The Ohio Arts Council is the second largest and most active arts agency in the United States. The icon is based on the easily recognizable shape of Ohio, visually activated by the calligraphic brush rendering to suggest the aggressive stance of the Council. Notice how the rendering (on the right) implies the Council's activity extends beyond the state border.* (Waters Design Associates)

FIGURE 6–89. USS Constitution 200. (Favermann Design)

USS Constitution 200

FIGURE 6–90.
*Portland International
Film Festival.*
(Sandstrom Design)

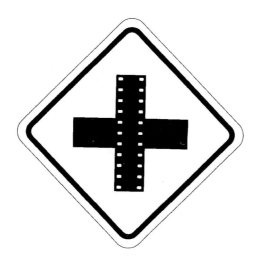

FIGURE 6–91. *If you
had to guess the name
of this company, what
would be your answer?
The pictogram nature
of this logo makes it
easy: Crossroad Films.*
(Pentagram NY)

FIGURE 6–92. *Cedric Lisney & Associates is a building and landscaping architectural group in the United Kingdom.* (Pentagram London)

FIGURE 6–93. *Streetscape, UK specializes in street furniture.* (Pentagram London)

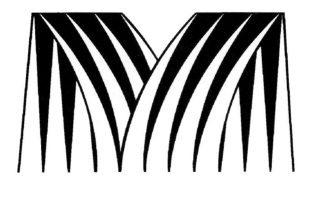

FIGURE 6–94. *Grass blades part to form the* M *for Mitch's Landscaping's logo.* (Gardner Design)

FIGURE 6–95. *La Scaux Restaurant.* (VanderByl Design)

FIGURE 6–96. *Various coffee products are alluded to in this striking logo for Third Coast Coffee Roasting Company.* (Tocquigny Advertising and Design)

Third Coast Coffee
R O A S T I N G   C O M P A N Y

FIGURE 6–97. *The Good Diner Restaurant. Sometimes, an unaffected, almost goofy approach works, but only when it truly reflects the character of the clients business.* (Pentagram NY)

FIGURE 6–98. *Los Gatos Cats Festival is a street fair designed to bring business into the downtown district. A cat show and crafts fair are just a part of this annual event.* (Max Davis Company N.A.)

FIGURE 6–99. *American Zoo and Aquarium Association is an organization that advocates habitat protection and captive management of endangered species.* (Grafik Communications Inc.)

FIGURE 6–100. *This logo for the Tennessee Aquarium in Chattanooga works well in multicolor applications as well as black and white and single color.* (Chermayeff & Geismar Inc.)

FIGURE 6–101.
*Med-Access, a medical
information and
retrieval company.*
(Brinkley Design)

FIGURE 6–102.
*Breaking apart a
capsule results in an
interesting* L *for Landa
Pharmaceutical, set
inside a "pill."*
(Pentagram NY)

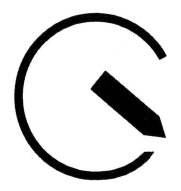

FIGURE 6–103. *Design icons form the G for Garma Design.* (Garma Design)

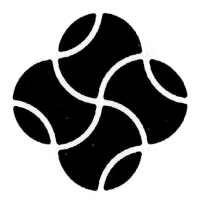

FIGURE 6–104. *These tennis balls overlap to form a T for the Tennis Training Center.* (UCI Inc.)

FIGURE 6–105.
*Thomas Hayward
Auctioneers.* (Pentagram)

FIGURES 6–106,
6–107. *Two very
different, yet very
effective approaches
for portraying the
same business
category. Stephen T.
Bennion (6–106)
builds fine furniture,
while John Boone
designs and sells it.*
(6–106 Smit Ghormley Lofgreen; 6–107
Waters Design
Associates)

6–107

6–106

FIGURE 6–108. *The Fashion Center, a business improvement district for New York City's garment industry, needed a logo that would stand out when applied to banners, etc., along the city's busy streets. Simplicity is key to this solution's visibility; still, it manages to incorporate wit.* (Pentagram NY)

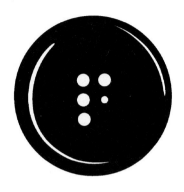

FIGURE 6–109. *One prime example of a mark that readily conveys the company's name as well as its business.* (Mires Design)

FIGURE 6–110. *Persimmon Books' logo not only implies a persimmon tree and book but the tree of knowledge, as well.* (Pentagram NY)

FIGURE 6–111. *Thorn EMI is a home security system.* (Pentagram London)

FIGURE 6–112. *This deconstructed "room" forms a creative mark for Interiors, an interior space planning consultancy.* (Gardner Design)

FIGURE 6–113, 6–114.
*Alki Bakery's stylish,
yet simple logo
communicates
effectively in a wide
variety of applications.*
(Hornall Anderson
Design Works)

6–113

6–114

FIGURE 6–115. *Developing logos for other creatives can lead to some of the more interesting identities, as the client is likely to be very educated regarding the value of good design and willing to let you develop truly innovative solutions. At the same time, creatives can be among your more challenging assignments, for the same reasons. This logo is for Renee Comet Photography.* (Bruce Morgan)

FIGURE 6–116. *A woven P says Polyfibres Inc.* (Weller Institute for the Cure of Design)

The Businessperson's Guide to Great Logos

7

While this book has addressed designers directly throughout, it is not for designers only. Anyone who must deal with developing a company's logo or identity system, in businesses both large and small, can gain valuable insight from knowing how effective logos are created and how they can help your company distance itself from competitors.

The following information is provided to better acquaint business people with some of the standard benefits of design and general practices of design professionals. It is by no means a thorough investigation of the profession, but it should enable you to have a very basic understanding of design and its language, thus facilitating your working relationship with a designer throughout the intricate process of developing and maintaining your new identity.

Finding the Perfect Design Partner

Companies often have an attorney, accountant, advertising agency, public relations, or insurance professional as part of their operations team, whether these people are on staff or are outside consultants. A professional designer likewise is a valuable partner to any business.

It follows, then, that the first step in any new logo development program is developing a good working relationship with a designer. So, before you start the planning process, look around for a highly competent graphic designer to work with—that special creative person who can ultimately implement the design of your optimum logo. Both of you will be the essential players in the design development process. And if more than one person in your company is going to be assisting in the selection of the final design, it is imperative that all participate in the planning, so bring them in on the process. If everyone feels they've been a part, the solution you and your designer offer is much more likely to be accepted company-wide.

To put the professional relationship you should have with your designer in simple perspective, working with a designer is like working with an accomplished chef. They both work with ingredients in the proper proportions and order, plus add their own special insightful touches to create a masterpiece — whether it be your credibility-based logo or Beef Wellington. Criteria-based logo design is no different than criteria-based (gourmet) cooking. It just takes a lot more work and a lot longer to get to the end result. Yet the product is certain to be more eagerly accepted than a hasty, ill-planned logo, just as is a home-baked pie from a talented chef over a ready-made version from the grocer's freezer.

How to Find a Designer

Conduct your search for a graphic designer as painstakingly as if you were seeking a permanent business partner, because that's exactly how this person should be viewed. A good way to find the perfect design partner who will make your logo dream a reality is to use your new knowledge of credibility persuasion.

When you see work that you judge to be especially successful in expressing another company's credibility, find out who the designer was. You might simply ask the companies whose logos you admire. Another way is to look in graphic design magazines or reference books in your city library.

Your next step is to contact the designer whose work you are interested in and set up a meeting. At the meeting you will want to:

- Review the designer's portfolio (samples) of work done for other clients.

- Learn the designer's approach to graphic design; that is, does the designer actually design with credibility persuasion objectives and criteria? Does he or she understand the communication principle of credibility persuasion and does he or she understand the process of designing a logo with credibility attributes?

- Discuss the objectives of your logo/marketing communications system.

- Discuss your planning approach and your philosophy based upon your understanding of credibility persuasion.

- Show your present logo implementation wall if you have taken the project to that first step in the planning stage.

- Walk the designer around your office and/or business. As each area of public contact is an opportunity for marketing communication, the designer might have some further suggestions on ways to apply your new logo that he or she can incorporate into the implementation program they develop for your new identity. (Don't ask them to give this information out for free during your selection process, however.)

If necessary, repeat this process with two, three, or several designers whose work you admire. With your new knowledge, you should be able to limit the field to a real design professional who will be well worth his or her design fee.

How to Review a Proposal

When you think you are comfortable with a designer, ask for a **proposal**. You may need one or two to cover different phases of your logo implementation plan. Phase One normally covers logo development only. Phase Two would cover the implementation of some or all of the items in your marketing communications system. If it is a simple implementation effort, one proposal is usually sufficient. The following are the normal ingredients in a design proposal, and what you should be looking for when you review them.

1. *Scope of the assignment.* This is a statement of objectives. This statement is broad and will be further defined in the planning stage. Study this to determine the designer's understanding of both the assignment and your expectations.

2. *Work to be performed.* This is an outline of the steps taken through to final presentation. Included is planning/development of design criteria, preliminary design development, preliminary meeting(s), design refinement of promising alternatives, and final presentation of the recommended solution. When it comes to how the logo might look in implementation on your stationery, signs, or company vehicles, the designer would show examples (rather than actual products or drawings). With large companies, a dozen or so examples would be prepared as part of the final presentation. Do not expect the designer to develop any logo sketches at this point. Most designers consider that "spec" work, and will likely refuse to do it. (Many have been bitten by clients who took their proposal ideas and hired another firm to produce them.)

3. *Designer fees and payment schedule.* The fees structure might be for the total assignment, or by phases such as planning, design development, or implementation. Fees might be given in a range. Likewise, designers often include a clause in the proposal stating that if the project cost goes beyond a certain set point over the estimate (ten percent beyond is a standard) they must inform you before proceeding further. One other thing: If you are planning on using the logo in a direct-profit manner—such as on T-shirts or other items that you intend to sell for profit—your designer may ask for royalties. That is because you have crossed the line of normal usage, and stepped into the licensing arena. Discuss this with your designer in advance. (It is possible to do a buyout of the design, but be prepared to pay significantly more than if you were using it for identity purposes only.)

It's also not unusual for the designer's "out of pocket" or "re-imbursable" expenses to be billed with an additional markup for overhead and handling (usually 15 to 20 percent). If so, you should have an agreement that the designer obtain advance approval for expensive items (and, likewise, agree on the amount that will determine "expensive"). Receipts for such expenses should be provided to you. The designer should also outline when he or she expects to be paid. Many expect a third of the amount at the project's onset, another third at the project's middle juncture, and the final upon handing over the final design. If all is agreeable, both parties sign the estimated cost.

4. *Change orders.* These are always prepared by the designer and approved by the company manager, then signed by both parties.

5. *References.* This is important. The designer should list present and/or former clients with names, addresses, and telephone numbers. Investigate. If not included in the proposal, you should ask.

6. *Implementation.* Implementation of specific items on your implementation wall is usually included in Phase Two of the proposal. If there are many aspects to putting your logo to work, the proposal may have a Phase Three and Phase Four. If there are few, fees are covered in the design development phase. Obviously, items with the greatest exposure or impact potential should be implemented first. Cost of implementation will also determine priorities.

7. *Sign-off.* If all looks satisfactory, the proposal is signed and dated by both parties.

Now you and your designer are prepared to work together to plan, create, judge, and implement your effective new logo to help you acheive the desired company goals.

Glossary: The Language of Logo Design

Acronym/monogram logos Those made up of the first letter of each word in the company's or product's name, such as IBM or RCA.

Corporate identity (corporate imagery) A controlled visual expression of a company's character and personality.

Credible Believable; trustworthy and expert.

Credibility trait statement A written statement outlining a business' (or person's) credible attributes and personality traits. This is often one of the first steps taken by designers in researching a client's new identity.

Design standards manual A guidebook (often loose-leaf so it can be added to as needed) outlining the logo's reproduction guidelines and its application in all possible situations.

Font A complete set of alphabets relating to one size of typeface. This normally includes uppercase and lowercase roman, plus the various typestyles (italics, boldface, condensed, etc.).

Graphic design The art of arranging text and/or various icons in a manner that facilitates the conveyance of a message.

Infringement When one logo looks too much like another company's and could result in confusion by viewers as to whose mark it is, whether done intentionally or not. The courts use several set points in determining whether a logo actually infringes on another.

Logotype The name of a company or product designed in a specific way that is used as a trademark.

Line-extension A marketing technique in which a new product is spun off another, promoted by making use of the original product's name and success.

Logo power When a logo is designed in such a way that it embodies and reflects the company credibility traits, that is, "expertise" and "trustworthiness." The final solution will also be "appropriate," "interesting," and "unique." The credibility-based logo is then an effective marketing communication, which helps achieve a company's goals.

Name-only logos Those consisting solely of the business's name, such as Mobil or Xerox.

Name/symbol logos Those consisting of the company name paired with a symbol, such as the NBC peacock logo. (Also called a **signature**).

PANTONE Color Matching System ® A color system in standard use by designers and printers that allows them to specify consistent color-matching across printing inks, papers, and pens. Each PANTONE ink has a color swatch and number associated with it for reference.

Perception The way others view you or you view others, whether that view is reality or not.

Positioning Following a carefully devised marketing and promotional plan that will enable you to establish a niche in a certain market arena. A credibility-based logo is the energy for positioning.

Signature A logotype combined with a mark (symbol) used as a trademark.

Totally credible company One that maximizes its business expertise and trustworthiness in the way it operates, managing employees by a company value system that leads to product or service excellence.

Typeface An alphabet created for the purpose of reproduction.

Type style The way in which an alphabet is set: italics, boldface, condensed, expanded, etc.

Suggested Reading

Biedermann, Hans. *Dictionary of Symbolism: Cultural Icons and the Meaning Behind Them.* New York: Facts on File, 1992.

Dormer, Peter. *Design Since 1945.* London: Thames and Hudson Ltd., 1993.

Key, Wilson Bryan, PhD. *The Age of Manipulation: The Con in Confidence, the Sin in Sincere.* Lanham, MD: Madison Books, 1993.

Livingston, Alan and Isabella. *The Thames and Hudson Encyclopaedia of Graphic Design + Designers.* London: Thames and Hudson Ltd., 1992.

Meggs, Philip B. *A History of Graphic Design*, 2nd ed. New York: Van Nostrand Reinhold, 1992.

Morgan, Hal. *Symbols of America.* New York: Viking, 1986.

Murphy, John and Michael Rowe. *How to Design Trademarks & Logos.* Cincinnati, OH: North Light Books, 1988.

Ries, Al and Jack Trout. *Positioning: The Battle for Your Mind.* New York: McGraw-Hill, 1986.

Robbins, Harvey A. *How to Speak and Listen Effectively.* New York: American Management Association, 1992.

Stanley, Richard E. *Promotion: Advertising, Publicity, Personal Selling, Sales Promotion*, 2nd ed. Englewood Cliffs, NJ: Prentice-Hall, 1982.

Wurman, Richard Saul. *Information Anxiety.* New York: Doubleday, 1989.

Figure Credits

6–42 *Time Warner*
Chermayeff & Geismar Inc.

6–43 *Waters Design Associates Inc.*
Waters Design Associates Inc.
Design Director: John Waters
Designers: John Waters,
Jeanine Guido

6–44 *Electro Scan*
Malcolm Grear Designers

6–45 *French Paper Co.*
Charles S. Anderson Design
Company

6–46 *Dur-O-Tone (French Paper Co.)*
Charles S. Anderson Design
Company

6–47 *Conservation Corps*
VanderByl Design
San Francisco, CA
Designer: Michael VanderByl

6–48 *League of Conservation Voters*
Grafik Communications Inc.
Alexandria, VA
Creative Director: Judy Kirpich

6–49 *Tropical Forest Foundation*
Grafik Communications Inc.
Creative Director: Judy Kirpich

6–50 *NEPCO*
Malcolm Grear Designers

6–51, 6–52 *Koc Museum and
University*
Chermayeff & Geismar Inc.

6–53 *Caribbean Heartburn
(American Heart Association)*
Firehouse 101 Art + Design
Designer: Kirk Richard Smith
Illustration: Kirk Richard Smith
Creative Contributor: Tuesday
Trippier

6–54 *Ocoee River Olympics Site*
Favermann Design
Designers: Mark Favermann,
Paul Cunningham, Grisela
Basualdo

6–55 *Sprint Canoe Olympics Trials*
Favermann Design
Designers: Mark Favermann,
Paul Cunningham, Grisela
Basualdo

6–56 *Slalom Canoe Olympic Trials*
Favermann Design
Designers: Mark Favermann,
Paul Cunningham, Grisela
Basualdo

6–57 *Mandarin Oriental*
Pentagram
Designers: New York office

6–58 *Roadrunner Records*
Smit Ghormley Lofgreen Inc.
Phoenix, AZ
Designer: Art Lofgreen

6–59 *Sierra Man*
Charles S. Anderson Design
Company

6–60 *Sierra Bear*
Charles S. Anderson Design
Company

6–61 *50 Years of Kicks*
Favermann Design
Designers: Mark Favermann,
Paul Cunningham

6–62 *World Cup USA '94*
Pentagram
Designers: New York office

6–63 *The Edge*
Charles S. Anderson Design
Company

6–64 *Radio Ranch*
Pentagram
Designers: New York office

6–65 *Oahu Racquet Club*
Nick Kaars and Associates Inc.
Honolulu, HI
Designer: Nick Kaars

6–66 *Mr. & Mrs. Aubrey Hair*
Pentagram
Designers: New York office

6–67 *PANTONE Color Matching
System*
Charles S. Anderson Design
Company

6–68 *Hawaii Seafood*
Eric Woo Design Inc.

Honolulu, HI
Designers: Eric Woo, Jack Elder

6–69 *Truth Decay*
Firehouse 101 Art + Design
Designer: Kirk Richard Smith
Illustration: Kirk Richard Smith
Copywriter: John Shuttleworth

6–70 *Endymion Ensemble*
Pentagram
Designers: New York office

6–71 *House of Music*
Bud Linschoten

6–72 *Theatre Square*
VanderByl Design
Designer: Michael VanderByl

6–73 *The Becker Group*
Grafik Communications Ltd.
Creative Director: Judy Kirpich

6–74 *Travis Construction*
Pentagram
Designers: New York office

6–75 *J. Sadler Co.*
Harrisberger Creative
Virginia Beach, VA
Designer: Lynn Harrisberger

6–76 *Ferreteria El Potosino*
Machuca Design
Designer: Mauro Machuca

6–77 *Gamut Media*
Pinkhaus
Art Directors: Joel Fuller, Todd Houser
Designer: Todd Houser

6–78 *Sony E-TV*
Charles S. Anderson Company

6–79 *Century Hawaii Realty*
Bud Linschoten

6–80 *Bauer Skates*
Pinkhaus
Art Director: John Norman
Designer: John Norman

6–81 *Nike Football*
Charles S. Anderson Design Company

6–82 *Fox River Paper*
Pentagram
Designers: New York office

6–83 *Wichita Industry and Services for the Blind*
Gardner Design
Designer: Bill Gardner

6–84 *ARK Fence*
Gardner Design
Designer: Bill Gardner

6–85 *Bergelectric Corp.*
The Weller Institute for the Cure of Design
Oakly, UT
Designer: Don Weller

6–86 *Faulkner Institute for Eye Care and Surgery*
Bud Linschoten

6–87 *Nike Know Yourself*
Max Davis Company N.A.
Santa Cruz, CA
Designer: Max Davis

6–88 *Ohio Arts Council*
Waters Design Associates Inc.
Design Director: John Waters
Designer: Bob Kellerman

6–89 *USS Constitution 200*
Favermann Design
Designers: Mark Favermann, Paul Cunningham, Grisela Basualdo

6–90 *Portland International Film Festival*
Sandstrom Design
Portland, OR
Designer: Steve Sandstrom

6–91 *Crossroads Films*
Pentagram
Designers: New York office

6–92 *Cedric Lisney & Associates*
Pentagram
Designers: London office

6–93 *Streetscape*
Pentagram
Designers: London office

6–94   *Mitch's Landscaping*
       Gardner Design
       Designer: Bill Gardner

6–95   *La Scaux*
       VanderByl Design
       Designer: Michael VanderByl

6–96   *Third Coast Coffee Co.*
       Tocquigny Advertising and
       Design
       Austin, TX
       Designer: Mark Brinkman

6–97   *The Good Diner*
       Pentagram
       Designers: New York office

6–98   *Los Gatos Cats Festival*
       Max Davis Company N.A.
       Designer: Max Davis

6–99   *American Zoo & Aquarium
       Association*
       Grafik Communications Inc.
       Creative Director: Judy Kirpich

6–100 *Tennessee Aquarium*
       Chermayeff & Geismar Inc.

6–101 *MedAccess*
       Brinkley Design
       Charlotte, NC
       Designer: Leigh Brinkley

6–102 *Landa Pharmaceuticals*
       Pentagram
       Designers: New York office

6–103 *Garma Design*
       Garma Design
       Honolulu, HI
       Designer: Alfredo Garma

6–104 *Tennis Training Center*
       UCI Inc.
       Honolulu, HI
       Designer: Ryo Urano

6–105 *Thomas Hayward Auctioneers*
       Pentagram
       Designers: Austin, TX office

6–106 *Stephen T. Bennion Furniture
       Maker*
       Smit Ghormley Lofgreen
       Design
       Designer: Art Lofgreen

6–107 *John Boone*
       Waters Design Associates Inc.
       Design Director: John Waters
       Designer: Colleen Syron

6–108 *The Fashion Center*
       Pentagram
       Designers: New York office

6–109 *Magic Carpet Books*
       Mires Design
       Designer: Jose Serrano

6–110 *Persimmon Books*
       Pentagram
       Designers: New York office

6–111 *Thorn EMI*
       Pentagram
       Designers: London office

6–112 *Interiors*
       Gardner Design
       Designer: Bill Gardner

6–113 *Alki Bakery logo*
       Hornall Anderson Design
       Works
       Art Director: Jack Anderson
       Designers: Jack Anderson,
       David Bates

6–114 *Alki Bakery corporate ID*
       Hornall Anderson Design
       Works
       Art Director: Jack Anderson
       Designers: Jack Anderson,
       David Bates

6–115 *Renee Comet Photography*
       Bruce Morgan
       Washington, D.C.

6–116 *Polyfibres Inc.*
       The Weller Institute for the
       Cure of Design
       Designer: Don Weller

Color section

C–1—C–7 *Ellerbe Becket computer
         show*
         Hall Kelley Inc.©

C–8   *City of Phoenix logo*
       Smit Ghormley Lofgreen
       Design
       Designer: Brad Ghormley

C–9 *San Francisco International Film Festival*
Primo Angeli Inc.
San Francisco, CAC–10
Ultra Lucca Delicatessen
Primo Angeli Inc.

C–10 *Ultra Lucca Delicatessan*
Primo Angeli, Inc.

C–11 *Cochran Char*
Bud Linschoten

C–12 *Southern California Gas Co*
Sussman/Prejza Design & Co. Inc.
Designer: Deborah Sussman

C–13 *Sister Red*
Pinkhaus
Art Director: Tom Sterling
Designer: Tom Sterling

C–14 *Starbucks Coffee*
Hornall Anderson Design Works
Art Director: Jack Anderson
Designers: Jack Anderson, Julia Lock, David Bates, Julia LaPine

C–15 *Starbucks Frappuccino*
Hornall Anderson Design Works
Art Director: Jack Anderson
Designers: Jack Anderson, Julia Lock, Jana Nishi, Julie Keenan, Julia LaPine, Mary Chin Hutchison

C–16 *NBC*
Chermayeff & Geismar Inc.

C–17 *TBS logo*
Shimokochi/Reeves
Designers: Mamoru Shimokochi, Anne Reeves

C–18 *Sara Lee Olympic Partnership*
Pinkhaus
Art Directors: Joel Fuller, Claudia Kis
Designer: Claudia Kis

C–19, C–20 *The Masonry Company*
Smit Ghormley Lofgreen Design
Designer: Brad Ghormley

C–21 *Pacific Harbor Travel*
Max Davis Company N.A.
Designer: Max Davis

C–22, C–23a, C–23b *Rock 'n' Roll Hall of Fame*
Nesnadny + Schwartz

C–24 *Pepsi Stuff*
Pinkhaus
Art Director: Jon Norman
Designers: Jon Norman, Mark Cantor, Eric Pearle
Illustrators: Eric Pearle, Todd Houser
Photographer: Eric Pearle

C–25 *Lipton Tennis Tournament*
Pinkhaus
Art Director: Joel Fuller, Jon Norman
Designers: Jon Norman, Susy Lawson

C–26 *New York City AIDS Walk*
Drive Communications
Art Director: Michael Graziolo

C–27 *Nurture Our Diverse City*
Hall Kelley Inc.©
Designer: Michael Hall

C–28 *Hornall Anderson Design Works attitude board* Hornall Anderson Design Works

C–29 *Deleo Clay Tile*
Mires Design
Designer: Jose Serrano

C–30 *Snappers*
Pinkhaus
Art Director: Tom Sterling
Designer: Tom Sterling

C–31 *Players Inc.*
Grafik Communications Inc.
Creative Director: Judy Kirpich

C–32 *National Football League Players Association*
Grafik Communications Inc.
Creative Director: Judy Kirpich

C–33 *Pannikin*
Mires Design
Designer: Jose Serrano

C–34 *Corbis Web site announcement*
Hornall Anderson Design
Works
Art Director: Jack Anderson
Designers: Jack Anderson, John
Anicker, David Bates

C–35 *The New Victory Theater*
Chermayeff & Geismar Inc.

C–36 *United Way*
Saul Bass Associates
Art Directors: Saul Bass, Art
Goodman

Designer: Mamoru
Shimokochi

C–37, C–38 *Cuningham, Hamilton,
Quiter Architects
stationery/brochure*
Hall Kelley Inc.©
Designer: Michael Hall

C–39 *WeeCare*
Richards & Swensen
Salt Lake City, UT
Designer: Bill Swensen

C–40 *Marketing Man logo*
Shimokochi/Reeves
Designers: Mamoru
Shimokochi, Anne Reeves

Index